Amazon Seller Central Secrets

By Bruce Walker

Table of Contents

Welcome

Thank you for buying this book.

If you're looking to start your own business online and you're looking to get started with Amazon, then you came to the right place. If you want to make yourself a supplemental living or make this a full-time venue, then this book is for you.

I will show you how and I will show you the mistakes that I made when I started out on Amazon. Then I will show you how to do it better with what I have learned over the years.

But if you're buying this book because you want to get rich overnight, then return the book. If you think that you're going to buy this and you're going to be making $100,000 overnight, and you can quit your day job then return it. Go back to wherever you purchased this book, tell them you're not interested it's not what you thought and get a refund.

This is not going to be that type of a book. My method is not a quick get-rich-quick scheme; my method is hard work. My method is going to show you how to do things efficiently and better than I did. And I will show you how to make money while having a good time. All so you can have a more relaxed life and profitable lifestyle. If that's what you're looking for, then read on, and I'll teach you everything you need to know.

I thank you for purchasing this book and sit back, grab yourself something to make some notes with let's get started.

Bruce Walker

Chapter 1 The Beginning Of The End

Hi, my name is Bruce Walker; you may have read some of the other books that I have written over the past few years. If not then let me tell you that my goal is to help you succeed. I want you to create multiple streams of income; I don't tie myself down to one source of income as I did earlier in my life. I found out the hard way that that's the worst thing you can do. You set yourself up for failure.

But first, let me give you a little background on me. I worked for a large corporation; I was in middle management. I felt safe and comfortable; I was living the American dream. I had a house; I had two children and a beautiful wife. We had two cars and a new home with about 3 acres. We had two dogs and a cat, sometimes we had fish, and sometimes we had a hamster, it all depends on what the kids were in the mood for that month.

I had an excellent job like most people; I went to work, saw my boss and did my work to the best of my abilities. Someday hoping I would be the boss in this upper-level corporate heaven. I was the proverbial happy camper. My wife volunteered, she didn't have to work because my job paid very well. We were living what I considered the good life, and then one day it all came crashing down.

It was Friday on a cold winter's day as I walked into work from my car. As I walked in, I saw numerous of out-of-state cars in the executive parking area, which I thought was very unusual. I thought maybe they had sold the place or had some big investor come in. Perhaps they were there to sweep everything up. I didn't know what was happening, were we all going to get fired.

Once inside I see suits, lots of them with and with briefcases. After a few minutes, I started hearing rumors that were going around; the company was going to close. I thought that's impossible; they couldn't do that. But if they do its OK, they have sites all over the area. They have one 50 miles away so I can go work there and if I have to. They have the one at 70 miles away. I can go work there too, so it's all fine.

But it wasn't fine; it was my worst nightmare. They called me into the office and asked me if I am interested in taking a job in another state. I said why what is happening here, I love my job? They told me were closing this facility here and in fact, they were closing every other site in the 300-mile five-state area.

They told they had purchased a large office complex in South Carolina. South Carolina, I said that's over 600 miles away. No response. They asked are you interested. I said what do you mean. They said are you interested in going to South Carolina to work. I asked is that a bona fide offer. One gentleman whom I had never seen before looked at me; he pulled a piece of paper out of a folder and placed it in front of me and said sign here. He said a $25,000 pay increase, plus all expenses of the move if you go to South Carolina. But you have to sign it right now. I asked, can I call my wife. He said you're married? I said yes, and he pulled the paperback. No, you can't, we don't have time for chit-chat. No phone calls, he said we need to know right now. I said, are you discriminating against me because I'm married? The man replied absolutely not. We know that if you have to talk about it, that might take maybe two, three, four days. We need to know right now because have a game plan to work with. We need to know who we can count on and who we don't need to worry about.

I shuddered at the thought. This was utterly ridiculous for me to have to decide without discussing with my wife. She didn't work, so that was not going to be an issue. But I had a house to sell. I have two children in school. The man looked at me and said I know what your thing but don't worry about it. He said we would take care your house, we will get you moved, and we will pay for all your expenses. We will get you a new place there for at least a year until you can sell your house her. He shoved the paper back over in front of me. I said look; I really need to discuss this with my wife. He pulled the paperback and said no. I said, so you are discriminating against me because I'm married. He said absolutely not we are a family company. We prefer married men, so they're not going to be prancing around with the staff.

However, we need to make a decision right now, who's going to be with us and who's going to be not with us. I said look I need just two minutes; I need to call my wife. I said, it sounds like a great deal and it was. They were offering me a $25,000 salary increase. And with the cost of living down there, that's a $40,000 salary increase maybe even $50,000. They were offering me a $50,000 bonus just for signing the paper and going with them. I said look I really need two minutes to talk my wife. The gentleman pulled the paperback. Now there was nothing in front of me.

In a few seconds he reached into his briefcase and pulled out another paper, I looked at the new paper. This was my severance package. It was three months' salary. It also included all my sick time, my vacation time, my personal time and all the holidays for the rest of the year. This would all come up to about a month and 1/2's worth of salary. I asked, so there's no discussion on this. He said no I'm sorry there is a discussion. The discussion is who's with us and who's not with us. It's been a long decision to do this move, and we want you to come with us. But if you can't, we need you to need to sign this. He shoves the paperback. He said it's your choice.

I looked at both papers and said I have to speak with my wife. He pulled the paper with the offer on it back and threw it in the trash. He said sign this while shoving the severance package paperwork back to me. Why was the other one thrown in the trash I thought? But in reality, I knew that was a done deal. I knew then I had no choice.

I looked at the paper; there was my three months' salary with my vacation time. We were talking almost five months of salary. It was well over $80,000 that they were just going to give me. I signed the paper and looked up. I said, "I don't know what to say." One of gentleman along with a manager that I had known for ten years stood up, both shook my hand and said you have been a valued employee. We really appreciate all you have done for us.

The executive then reached out and said here's my business card, if you need a reference for anyplace you give me a call. I will give you a top-notch reference. And I will tell them that the only reason you didn't take a position with our company is that it was such a long move. I said, "But that's the truth." He said yes so no one will hold that fact against you. I said, "So that's it?" He said yes that's it. You can take this paper down to the payroll department on the first floor, and they'll cut you two checks.

Once you're finished, you can go home. I asked if I could clean out my desk. They also said I could take anything you want on the desk. In fact, if you want to take the desk too. We will have this entire facility gutted by Monday so anything you want, you can take. We have no intention of moving anything except files due to the expense involved. Everything else will be simply trashed.

I thanked them and walked towards the door. I turned around and said goodbye. I started to walk out, I stopped and turned around. I asked what if I went home and talked to my wife, could I apply for a job in the South Carolina office? I really do think my wife would love South

Carolina. The CEO said yes you could do that, but by the end of today, all of the jobs will be filled. We have seven more offices that we are closing; we need to leave here by noon to spread ourselves around. If you don't take a job now, then those jobs will be filled by the end of the day.

That doesn't mean something else will not come up later, and you could apply for that position. I assure you would get preferential treatment but today's the end of the day for you. I shook my head and thanked them. They all again shook my hand on the way out told me I was a valued employee. They reminded me to call them if I needed anything. Then the president of the company again reiterated he would give me the best reference that anyone could do. He says he'll tell them that he would let me marry his daughter, that is how much he likes me. He said I don't have a daughter but he really would anyway if he had one. I smiled and said thank you again and just walked away.

I was shocked they had given me a sizable chunk of change to leave, and I could go start working someplace else right away. I was lost; I didn't know what to do. I went to my desk and sat down. I looked up and out into the office and saw other people with filled boxes heading for the door. The maintenance man was walking around handing out boxes to everyone. I decided I had to get started even as hard as it was going to be. This office had been my home now for so many years. I started taking down all my pictures. I took everything that I possibly could find loose, including paper my staple and even some paperclips. When I finished all that was left was my the office equipment, my desk, and my chair. They did tell me to take everything, otherwise, it would all be in the trash.

I looked at my chair and thought wow, this was over thousand dollars. It was bought for me because I was top salesperson last year. I asked the gentleman walking around who was part of maintenance if I could take the chair. He said you could take everything he said they're going to gut this place. And everything inside will be trashed, they've ordered 15 dumpsters for outside. He said so whatever you don't take is going in the dumpster. That being the case I took my trashcan and my shredder. I even took the copier. I asked the maintenance man if I could have some toner for the copier. He brought me down a whole case of them. There were 10 of them in there. He asked where is your car? I'll take them outside for you. I pointed to the large black Escalade outside. I said that's mine. He said it's good you've got a big truck.

He went out took my SUV and carried the toner out for me. He also took several boxes of blank white paper. It was about 50 reams. He came back into my office and took my boxes out. I've known this guy for ten years we were not buddies, but we knew each other. We talked in the lunchroom; we talked at company gatherings. He was a good guy, and he really took care of me that day.

I finished boxing up my things in the office; then Dan stopped by and again asked me if I needed anything else. He says I have a whole stock room full of supplies that will be trash if someone doesn't take them. He said I should take whatever I can for myself. There is a whole stock room down there, pencils, paper and tons more take whatever you want. I went down and walked in, and he's right the place was full to the ceiling. They said it was too expensive to move it, so they were going to trash it. I thought why not, I grabbed notepad's, paper, pencils, calendars. I grabbed everything I could shove into the two boxes that I had left. He gave me some ink pads and two more boxes to fill up. I started to grab everything I could that wasn't tied down. Or anything that I thought I could use, including some of the company coffee mugs.

When I finished my whole truck was filled up to the back, and I even put some supplies in the back seat. I shook his hand and offered him a $20 bill, and he said no Bruce, it is not needed. He said you had been a good guy and I really enjoyed working with you over the years. I gave him my card and said give me a call. I said the cell phone number there is mine. He handed me his card, and he says let's do lunch sometime. I again shook his hand and said thank you.

I walked back inside said goodbye to everybody; I passed out my business cards. I took one more look in my office to make sure there was nothing that I wanted to take. I would really love to have had the desk. On my way out I said to Dan the maintenance man, that I wanted the desk. He said I see your trucks full now, so I will have it out by the front waiting for you. But my word of warning if it's not out by Sunday at 5 pm it will be trashed. He said they'll take it and crush it.

He said he would have the entire stock room out on the walkway for everyone. Take whatever you can or need, if not it will all go to waste. I took one look again at my former place of employment and then slid up into my SUV. I drove slowly down the long drive almost wanting to cry.

It was early, and I made it home around two in the afternoon. No rush hour traffic today for sure. Now, what do I say to wife? When I walked in my wife looked surprised and asked what was going on. Why was I home so early? Why was I home so soon? I said call the babysitter and let's go out for dinner. She said what's wrong. I said call the babysitter get dressed for dinner. She went quietly but not happy and proceeded to get dressed. I went up shaved and took a shower. I kind of felt dirty after all of this.

When I came downstairs, I could see the babysitter had arrived at about the same time kids got home from school. We kissed and hugged them and told him we'd see them later and we were going out for dinner. I said maybe we would go someplace on Saturday. I know there's an indoor water park in the mountains. Perhaps we would go there and stay the whole weekend. This brought excitement to their drab voices.

I took the wife out to a very nice restaurant for dinner or a late lunch. She said, " All right Bruce what the hell's going on?" I said the company closed today. She asked what did you say? I said yes the company closed today they are moving to South Carolina. She said so all the stuff in the back of your truck that you were emptying into the garage is from your work?. I said yes all this is stuff is what I could take from the office. I took all I could carry. They tell me by Monday it will be some kind of new storage facility. And everything has to go, and it's too expensive to move it all. We, the employees can take it all, or it will all be trashed. They will just throw it all away, so I took all I thought I could use.

She asked did they offer you a job at the new place? I said yes they did. She asked, and you didn't take it. I said it's in South Carolina almost 700 miles away; her mouth dropped to the floor. She said, "What are we going to do Brian?" I looked at her as I kissed her hand then I kissed her on the lips, and I said, "I don't know."

But they gave me two checks. I pulled them out and said the smaller was my vacation time, all my personal days and sick days. The larger one is my severance package. She looked at them, and she quickly calculated them. It was $89,856, almost 90,000 dollars. A smile came on her face but quickly disappeared. Then she asked how long will this last. I said well we have quite a bit of savings and this will certainly tide us over for six months easily. If we clampdown little bit, it'll probably tide us over for a year or more until I can find a new job. I said, but the whole job situation kills me. I worked for these people for 15 years; I put my life into them it really kills me.

Now she was consoling me because she could see I was upset. She could see I was depressed about the whole thing and she asked what are we going to do Brian. I don't want you to go back to another company and have this happen again. I agreed that then I would be on the doorstep again, and I would be too old probably to get a job someplace as I would be close to 60 then. She looked at me, and she said why don't you use some of the money to start your own business. Then you will be the boss. I looked at her, and I said you know that's a good idea. I said they fired me; now I will fire them. I will fire my boss to be my own boss. I would be my own master I'm not going let this happen to me again.

She said so what kind of business are you going to start? I said sales, of course, I know sales, I know marking, I know analytics. This is what I did for a living for this company. I was the best salesperson they ever had. I know how to analyze things. I said I'm going take several weeks to look at everything and analyze what the best solution is. If I do the job that I did for them, then I can make this work. They didn't pay me enough for the money I made them. I made all this money for this company, and they just threw me on this doorstep. I'm going to make more money than that for myself.

Now I was just ranting, but she could see my sadness and sorrow had turned to happiness. She said I don't know whether it's the alcohol or that's you talking, but I love it. We stopped talking about this nightmare and finished our dinner. When we went home, I had a new outlook on life. Be Your Own Boss. This is my new motto. No more being a slave to the corporate world.

Later that night I took the truck with one of my friends and drove back to the office. There on the sidewalk was my desk. It was sitting right out there along with about 10 or 15 other boxes of supplies and a file cabinet. Along with file the file cabinet, there was also another office chair. It was brand-new in the box and never opened. I really didn't even get a chance to look at all the stuff. I just pulled up and started loading everything I could. My friend helped me with the boxes and loading up the desk. Once the truck was loaded, we headed for home leaving piles of good equipment and supplies right there on the sidewalk. When we arrived home, we unloaded all of it in my garage.

Joe and I then went to sit out on the back deck. It was about 9 pm now; I put something on the grill to barbecue. We ate, had a few drinks and we talked for a couple of more hours. We brainstormed with some of the things I was thinking about doing. Joe is a great guy, but most of it was over his head. He works for a utility company. But he really hasn't worked for the last ten years. He drives around and looks busy. He's a union guy. Not that I'm against unions, but he told me how much he worked at not working because he knew he couldn't be fired. He was 30 years there. He said he was sorry and if he could do anything let him know. It is great to have good supporting friends.

After Joe went home that night, I simply couldn't sleep. I laid there and thought about how crazy this must sound to Joe. Seriously how stupid it seems to me when I look at it objectively. Leaving a good job and starting a business from nothing. Am I nuts? The answer is resounding YES!!

Next morning I ran back out to the office, I found other desks also just sitting there. One was even better than mine; I found a couple of folding tables and some folding chairs. I grabbed those, and there were also piles and piles and boxes outside. I found a brand-new filing cabinet and three more chairs that were brand-new in the box. I saw more office supplies. I felt like to make two or three runs back and forth. I wish I had brought my trailer. I grabbed everything I could shove into the SUV and took off one home and unloaded it all. Joe saw me and came over to help, and I told him that there was a lot more stuff out there. If he wanted some of the supplies to go there and help himself. I said you could take my trailer if you want. He said he would do that later.

When I arrived home on Sunday after the weekend away, I night I found out that he did go there and fill up the whole trailer full of things. He brought it all back to my house and parked in front. He took only a few things for himself. I had left by then, and he knew I had taken off with the kids for some downtime. I needed to think, so he did all the grunt work for me. It was kind of nice of him, and I really appreciated that. But we had headed off to Great Wolf Lodge to spend the weekend by the time Joe brought in the trailer so we didn't know.

One the way to the resort I spent the entire time thinking. Every time someone would say something to me, I would have to ask them to repeat it again. I was totally engrossed in my own thoughts. I really didn't know what to think, but I had some ideas. I wanted to do sales, and I wanted to make a good life out of this. I wanted not to be tied to one spot anymore. I don't want to tie myself to one company anymore. I don't want to put all my eggs in one basket.

Had I not been in the position where I was, with the knowledge I had, I would be sitting on the doorstep like hundreds of other employees. Or like thousands are right now. They are all sitting on the doorstep and wondering what the heck they're going to do next week for their meals. What they're going to do for their family. I was determined not to let that happen again. Fire my boss, be my own boss that is the ticket. I want to be my own master; no one can tell me what to do anymore, or tell me how I should thin or how they think I should do it better. If they can do it better than they should be doing it themselves.

But now for my downtime, it was wonderful. The water park was great. It was still a little chilly outside from spring but still very nice. However, my mind was not there. I really wanted to get something in my head, so I could start figuring out what was going to be the right thing to do. What can I sell; I really have nothing except office supplies. And I really don't want to sell those things. Although I do have quite a bit now. I brainstormed Saturday night after the kids went to sleep. My wife was hanging over me and worried that I was not getting enough sleep. I said no I need to come up with an idea and I need to come up with it now. I need to get started on manipulating and getting my thoughts turned into actions so I can get things to work out.

While searching the internet a menu popped up, it was something on Amazon that I had looked at a couple of weeks ago. The message said hey are you still looking for this? Look now it's on sale!! It was a computer did I need one still? Not really I said out loud, I looked around realizing I said it out loud. But no one heard me since everyone was asleep.

I didn't need a computer because I took 12 computers from work six of them brand-new in the box. I couldn't sell them because they were already opened but how can I put them to use? I ran all scenarios through my head while searching online doing research. I kept watching the Amazon ads pop up here and there. I watched the Google ads pop up here and there. Suddenly it came to me that most of the sellers and most the things I see are people just like me. Well not like me they have their own stores. But they are individual people or are small companies. I assume they are small because they don't have a lot of inventory when I look at their entire list. Why don't I sell something on Amazon?

I started searching for information on how to sell on Amazon and how to make a living selling on Amazon. I found every book about selling on Amazon. I took in all the information and then I sat back to look at everything I could imagine. My mind was filled with questions about where to find the sources to buy things. What am I going to buy first to sell? Where do I store this stuff? What do I do now? Then I went to Amazon to start reading their policies on how to become a seller. I found out that Amazon limits you to one selling account. Since I already have an Amazon account; maybe I could convert it to a selling account right away. But wait that limits me to one selling account. What if something happens? I read so many stories here about people getting shut down by Amazon for doing this. I need to do this right now.

I went to lay down, but I couldn't sleep. I thought about it all night, laying there thinking about what to do, but it was late. I couldn't really stay up anymore, but I also couldn't go to sleep. I kept thinking about getting up texting myself notes then lying back down. And because I was restless for the night, the children were restless too. So I decided I'm going to lie back down in bed and go to sleep. Tomorrow's going to be another day. I fell asleep hugging my wife telling her I'd found the solution. I was going to start an Amazon business. She probably didn't hear me, but I kissed her and went to sleep anyway.

The next morning we woke, I said nothing about my ideas, and we went to the water park again. We had another wonderful time. We stayed there until almost 6 o'clock. With an hour and a half drive, not including the stop for dinner, we arrived at home. We all took showers. The children went to bed right away; they had school in the morning. It's about 9 o'clock now; I sat down at my computer at the new desk that I had brought in the garage. I set out to convert a portion of the garage into my new office and warehouse. I have nothing to sell yet, but I'm already calling it my warehouse.

I started researching things to buy, what sells. Trying to research and finding out as much as I could learn out about Amazon. How Amazon really works. I knew how Amazon worked on some things. I'd written a couple of books on selling and how to sell and also written a couple of children books. I know how that worked. And yes I do get royalties from them in. I do have a couple of other books that I'm working on at the time that are unfinished. But I just I just didn't have time with my full-time job. Now I have time. But the book that is published and the ones I would like to get published will not put food on my table in the long-term. Eventually, they will; maybe I'll become a famous writer, but right now is just something extra.

I went to the internet again and read everything I could find out about selling on Amazon. I found out where to get supplies, where to get things to sell. I walked around the garage looking for things that I could sell. Then I did my own research. That's what I do best. In my previous job, I did analytics for one of the largest retail companies in America. This was not Amazon but one pretty close to them. I was in middle management and had all this sales knowledge stuffed inside my head. I should be able to do this and make a living selling on Amazon. Keyword there is I should be able to do this. After researching, I realized how hard it was. And how easy it was to get kicked off Amazon for things that you didn't even know where wrong.

Now comes the hard part, getting on Amazon, keeping my nose clean and staying there. My family depends on this. Maybe yours will too.

Chapter 2 The Beginning Of The Book

Selling on Amazon is indeed like nothing you've ever done before. Maybe you've sold at a flea market. Maybe you had a yard sale or something similar to that but not exactly like the people Amazon. These people are very particular about how they want things. It's not like what you're used to even if you sold stuff on eBay or Amazon before. It is again an entirely different animal being a professional seller. And if you have sold on eBay, you will find that the eBay buyers are different. But it will still give you some good experience.

On Amazon, you will have to learn your customers and learn the way things work. By reading this book and by doing some research, you will be on your way. By living the experience here on Amazon after two or three months, you will live and breathe Amazon. You will know it so well you can go to sleep and think about your customers. You will think about your sales and think about what you can do better; it will become second nature to you.

One thing you must make sure you do if you don't give up you will get nasty customers, and you will need to deal with them. You will have a bad day when the printer won't work, or the computer does the Internet doesn't work. You may have to shut the computer down half a dozen times, and you still can't get I to see the printer. Even though you hold the printer right in front of the computer, it still doesn't see it. (that's a joke) There will be days when everything will go against you. When that happens, close the door and go out to the local coffee shop, or the local convenience store. Grab yourself a cup of coffee or cold soda, doughnut, fried chicken, candy bar or whatever you want and relax. Take a chill pill, drive down the road for a few minutes and then come back.

When you come back start everything all over again, shut everything down. Start out like you're coming in from the beginning of the day. Hopefully, you remembered to turn the computers off when you left. Now when you come back start everything up all over again, it seems like a new day. Chances are, everything works. If it doesn't, take a calm approach to getting everything to work properly. This way you'll find that your life is so much better so much calmer and relaxed.

Take time for yourself. The advantage of doing business and being your own boss is that you are your own master. You are no longer a slave to someone else; no one else is telling you what to do. You know how much money you need to make. You need to make a plan on how much you need to have versus how much you have to sell. You know where you need to be to feel comfortable taking the day off to go fishing, or go for a walk. Or maybe you want to lay around and watch old episodes of Gilligan's Island. So relax. That's the idea. No one's pulling your chain no one is telling you that you're late and they're going to fire you for being late.

The only way you'll know that you're having a bad problem is when you go to look at your bank account. If you have to write a check for the electric bill and you don't have enough money there. That's when you say oh goodness, but even then work all night if you have to. There have been times when I was starting this project, that I would put my wife and kids to bed early. Then I would go out in the garage to work until 2 o'clock in the morning to get things straightened out. I was so damned tired, but I did what I had to do. The next morning when I woke up, I had three or $400 in sales. I knew that that weekend or the next week I would have money in my account. That was a good feeling, hard work pays off now, and it pays directly to me!

By being your own boss is being your own master you put your destiny in your hands. Slack off, and you starve, work hard and then see the results. No one's telling you where, when, or what you need to do, work at your pace. But always remember that your family depends on you. Got it? So let's get to work.

Now a word for our sponsor. ME! Send me an email directly to my email, when you do that I will send you my wholesale list. This is a kick start for you. I am trying to get you on the road to success. By giving you a sneak peek at the list, I hope this will get you motivated. Hopefully, you can work later tonight if you want as you go through this book. I am sure you'll find many ways that motivate you here. This is to kick start you and drive you to success.

My sources, my secret sources that I will email you are sold on for $47 on ClickBank. I sell them day in and day out, and you are getting them for free here for reading this book. These wholesale sources will allow you to buy wholesale or less and sell on Amazon for profit. I sell this for $47, and now I'm giving them to you for free for purchasing this book.

Also if you ask and sign up for my mailing list, I will send you my secret letters for free. These are letters that I use to get myself out of trouble with Amazon. I use them to get feedback removed, and I'm going to give you for free. I sell these on ClickBank for $97, but you're getting them for free. You're getting over a hundred dollars' worth of my hard work and years of my struggles with Amazon for free. Now you don't have to struggle the way I did. You will also get my email. That way if you run across a problem you can't fix then you have my email to ask for help. Chances are I ran across this issue in my experience on Amazon, and I forgot to mention it. But if I forgot something, let me know, and I update the book and I will also send you a free gift. I'll then go back and edit my book and mention your name in my next book. So it's a win-win situation for us all. So sit back but don't relax. Please pay attention.

Get ready to learn how to Be Your Own Boss!!

Be your own master and no longer be a slave to anyone.

Email me direct at Bep@c-4.net

I will reply within 24 hours! And I will send you a free gift.

Enjoy the book!

Chapter 3 Your First Account

So know enough about me and how I got into this. Now it's time to teach you how to get on Amazon, sell and make money.

Be your own boss, fire your old boss. Be your own master, no longer listen to anyone, no one will control your destiny. Sounds exciting right? I know you're thinking how the hell is he going to do that? Right, watch and see.

But before we go on let's get one thing straight, this is not a get rich quick scheme. I know other people will tell you that you can do this 3 hours a day and make 20k per month. Yes, you can, ONCE you get things going and have the inventory and suppliers to back you up. This requires work, yes I said that four letter word, now I have to wash out my mouth with soap. If you think you will sit back and wait long enough and everything will be fine, then you will have wasted a lot of time. If you think everything will all be hunky-dory and peachy keen, then forget about it it's not going to happen. It will not happen. And if you think that's what is going to happen and you've gotten this far in the book, please return the book for a refund.

Please think seriously about what you're doing. Don't think that you're going to throw some things out there and become an instant millionaire. If this is your plan, then you have bought the wrong book. I'm not going to lie to you. I will do nothing but tell the truth here.

This all requires hard work; you are going to have to learn to be your own advertising executive. You are going to have to learn how to be your own marketer. You are going have to learn how to be your own customer service. You are going to have to learn how to be your own shipping department. You are going to have to learn how to place orders. You will need to learn to buy stock and be a buyer. You are going to learn how to be an expert negotiator. You are going to have to learn how to be each one of these. And you're going to have to become a specialist in each one of these fields. Trust me you will be a specialist by the time you finish as I did. Several years later you will be able to teach other people to do this because you've done it so much. You will sleep eat and dream this life.

You have to learn to do all these jobs. And you have to recognize that if you have limits in one of these, you may have to get outside help. But for now, you can do it all on your own. You may not be the best, but you are all you have right now.

You have to realize that at all these jobs you have to be your best. You may not be the best but your all you have right now, so you have to work with what you have. Eventually, you may be able to hire some additional staff. Maybe you can hire some people off of fiver.com to do some marketing for you and to go on and post them blogs about you. Or you can find someone to post some different comments here and there to make sure that people see you and see your store. It's all about you, and it's all about what you want to get out of this. If you want to sit back and relax then you should go back to that cushy job at the corporate office. Then you can relax and hope everything will be okay.

Please return the book with no problems. No hard feelings from me, none whatsoever, and I wish you could see the expression on my face. I am sincere absolutely 100%. When I say that I will have no hard feelings I mean it because I am not going to promise you a miracle. I will tell you the truth. This all requires hard work. This all requires you get out and do things and if you don't think you can you're capable of doing it then don't. Why start and then say hey I failed, don't even do it. The only failure is going to be you not taking action. It will not be the system that failed. You didn't take action, and because of that, it didn't work out for you. You have to take action seize the moment, and if not then this system is not for you. Grab hold while you can and don't let go.

So if you're serious about doing this and you understand you have to work then let's do it. RIGHT NOW!!

You will need to make your first big decision almost right away when you decide to sell on Amazon. You need to decide if you want a Professional account or an Individual account. Both accounts charge you a percentage of the sale. I know you are starting on a shoestring budget and the individual account is better, to begin with in most cases. But after 40 sales on Amazon, you will pay the same amount as having a Professional account.

Keep in mind to win the buy box you need to be a Professional seller. I will explain later why this is very important. However, this is 39.95 per month. Most people begin with an Individual account. This is the least amount of money to start, but you do pay a bit more. All sellers pay 15%, but Individual sellers pay an additional 99¢ per sale.

As a Pro seller, you have many advantages. Such as you can apply to sell in restricted categories. You can upload inventory by using an excel spreadsheet that Amazon will provide you. You can also download reports, use Amazon click-through advertising and many other services. But the most significant advantage is getting a chance to compete for the buy box. And this is where almost 80% of the sales take place.

Now you think about that, and we will get to the setting up of your first account.

First, what you need to do you need to create yourself a business name, choose a name that people can remember and associate with your account. It can be anything you want if your name is Bob then try Bob's discount. Or if you are a Larry then Larry's discount. You can try Sam's discount, USA wholesale, USA liquidation or Bruce's Amazon account. I usually choose a name that reflects Amazon. Try Amazon Store New England. Something that you think is going to be catchy. So that people will get to know you. Don't use your last name; you want some level of anonymity. You don't want a customer calling you at home or asking to allow them to pick up something at your house. (I have had this happen.)

The next thing you need to do is make sure you use an IP that is not connected to your home personal account. Now you can use a cell phone and tether your phone to it, or get an extra IP. If you happen to live in a Comcast neighborhood where people have Xfinity you can log in and catch Xfinity Wi-Fi. Theoretically each time you log on to Xfinity with a different computer you get a different IP. I've tried it multiple times, and I always get a different IP. But you need to try it yourself to make sure. If your buying and selling account is the same, then you can skip this step. If you want to keep them separate then don't skip this. It will save you hassles later. See the back of the book for tips on getting a separate IP.

I am sure by now you have done enough research to know you can have only one account. That is true. Amazon does it. Amazon alone has the regular Amazon and Amazon warehouse deals. They even have others if you search for them. Ask, and they will allow it. Just put in a request stating your reason. If you have two completely different types businesses and they sell different items, ask Amazon for approval. If your companies are truly separate and they are owned by independent corporations or LLC's Amazon will allow it if you can prove a need. There are other ways to do this but, this is the safest way, and you have Amazon's blessing.

There is no problem having multiple Amazon accounts; Sears has an account. Kmart has multiple accounts. All of their subsidiaries have an account. Even though they're owned by the same holding company. So there's nothing wrong with you being the CEO of many companies and having many accounts. BUT you need to treat them as separate companies. And you need separate names. Separate IP addresses, separate business addresses, and SEPARATE COMPUTERS. Amazon drops cookies on your computer. If you ever use the same computer to log in to multiple accounts, YOU WILL BE blocked. And most likely lose all your accounts. Remember I speak from experience and have failed miserably. I have gone through all these troubles so that YOU WON'T HAVE TOO. Please heed my warning.

But always ask for Amazons approval first. If not you will be suspended and not allowed to have any account ever again. Heed my warning.

Again you want to start with one account. Choose a name that you would like. You can even register that name with the state. If you would like, it is not necessary since it's all going to be funneled into your account. When you do taxes, your accountant will tell you that each account must have its own schedule C. Keep this is mind. But don't take my word for it. I'm not a tax advisor. I'm telling you that each account you create is a separate business and you must keep it that way.

As a separate business, each account you create is a person or entity for IRS and Amazon purposes. What you have done is create an entity or an imaginary person it doesn't exist. You are a real person that controls these accounts, and you can never mix up the names between your accounts. No more than you want your next door neighbor coming in and using your house as his own. You must remember this.

When you create your first seller account, Amazon will ask you for an EIN or your SSN. Never, I repeat never, and I repeat never use your SSN. Go to IRS.gov and create a company name, use the same name as the one you have for your Amazon account. Never use your home address. I repeat never use your home address, use your work address or rent a postal box. Just use something different from your home address. Use the same address on your IRS form. You will have to match those addresses. The addresses need to match what the IRS has and what you use for AMAZON. It must match exactly.

What you have done is create an entity, a real person. Well, not a real person, but as far as in the computer world it's a real person. Amazon will need that information to verify that identity. So if you create more than one account, then you will need to do this for every seller account that you use. You cannot use the same ID or the same name or the same address. I rent the space at one of the local mailbox centers. They allow me to use apartment 489, apartment house 489, office 489, Suite 489. Anything I want as long as I have the correct street address. They are like mailboxes at the post office but more flexible. Any mailbox rental company seems to work fine. They are all over the place. You can spend anywhere from $10 a month to $40 a month, Just find the cheapest one or use your office address.

So as I said, you go to AmazonSellerCentral.com to create a seller account. It will ask you for your tax ID. They need to know who they're paying the money for from all the profits, the millions of dollars are going to make. Well not at first from Amazon but let's hope for the best. There's a box where it says check here if you have created your ID in the last 60 days. Check this box if you have9 it requires them to do an extra step to identify you. It only it takes about a minute. Make sure the address matches exactly what you used on your IRS form. If it is not exact Amazon will reject your tax form, and you have to start again. Print the IRS form so that you have a copy of it or save it as a PDF file. Be sure to keep a record of this in your filing cabinet.

Once this is done, you have a few settings to take care of on Amazon. Amazon needs your mailing address, and you will need to add a credit card to pay for shipping fees. You will also need to fill out a shipping template. This is how much you will charge for shipping. I charge 10.00 for shipping and then try to match prices as needed. Also, you need to decide if you want to ship to Canada and Mexico. All of these are completed in the setting area of seller central.

Once you've created your new Amazon account and now you have done all your homework you are ready to go. Now when I say this is a dedicated Amazon computer, it does not mean you can't use the computer for something else. But you can never go on to another Amazon account or any other account EVER! Trust me; I had an employee that went on my computer with their login and then they were banned. Amazon is heartless; they banned me too. It took forever to prove this person was not me.

If you don't have a spare computer that you can use, go to goodwill or buy one off of Amazon. Have it shipped to your house, wipe it or refresh it. Do whatever you have to do to install new software before you start using it. The computer must be clean before you can use it. It can never be associated with any other account. If so Amazon may by mistake associate this computer with another account. Not a good thing, like on Ghostbuster's crossing streams is a bad thing. It's a very bad thing, and something terrible will happen. Most likely your account could be banned from Amazon for life. I've seen people have that happen. There are ways to get reinstated or get around that, but why bother. Try to keep it clean and only cross that bridge unless you have to.

Are you ready to get started finally? Let's go for the next chapter now!

Chapter 4 My Search For Saleable Items

Once your account is up and running. You need something to sell. If you read the first chapter and took my free offer, you already have a list of where you can buy discount and surplus items. Some Items will be way below cost, so hopefully, you've already done that. Maybe you've done that and purchased your first items to list. If you haven't done that yet, then start your search as I did. Search at home! That is where I started. I walked around my garage looking for things to sell. I found a couple of old cameras I hadn't used, but I am sure they still had some value. I found a box of cell phones that as we've upgraded over the years. I didn't throw these things away; I kept thinking I would donate them, now I have donated them to my newest charity. ME!

Look around your house and see what you have. The first things I sold I found as I walked into my garage. I found things that I didn't need; I found a box of old phones, I found some old cameras that we didn't use. I found an old computer that I didn't need anymore. I found the motherboard from a computer that I didn't even remember

I had; It was outdated by 5 or 6 years. But you know what somebody buys all this stuff. I found some things I bought for the yard that I didn't need. Your house is a treasure trove, look for old Skis, helmets, etc., maybe books or old phones. Anything can be sold on Amazon if you want to sell it. You can find so many categories on Amazon, and it is easy to sell things on the platform. As I first started out I sold everything, all under one account

I took the items I had around the house and sold those as my primary source of inventory. The first item I listed was an old cell phone. It was amazing to find that people wanted some of these things. They are dinosaurs, but they still want them. When I searched on Amazon people were still buying these things amazingly. So I eventually listed a couple of old iPhone 2's and one iPhone 3 series. I don't know why people wanted them. Maybe for parts as one didn't even work. I also said that it didn't work and that it had a broken screen and still sold the thing for $40. It's amazing.

You can do this too, search high and low to find your stash of inventory. Once you have found your stash, sort these items into categories and condition. Once again, you need to make sure when you get ready to list that you know your inventory's' condition very well. Go to

AmazonSellerCentral.com and read CAREFULLY each description of the condition. After you have evaluated each item for its condition and its functionality, you can move to the next step.

Now sort these items by what has a UPC and what does not. You want to do the easy items first, then move on to more difficult items. That way you get to see the way it works and ease yourself into the art of Amazon. When listing your items, be accurate and never sugarcoat your listings. Your buyers will not like you, and your account will suffer. Also, make sure you don't need approval for any items you plan to list.

Some things that are listed on Amazon require approval first before you the seller can list them. I will explain later how to get approval for these items and some of the restricted categories. I will also tell you how to get proper invoices for Amazon. A proper invoice will show them that you purchased these things legally and have the right to sell them.

To keep it easily and straight in your mind, you need to develop a numbering system to sort everything. You can't throw it all in a box and hope to find; it doesn't work that way. I know I tried it. Get organized now, because when you have 3000 items, you will be suffering.

Eventually, you will need to have some type of tracking system. Perhaps like I did, maybe you have a better way. Your choice, I'm telling you how I did it. I create my inventory system by using the first three letters of my username for Amazon. Then I choose random numbers for the remaining portion of the stock number.

You can use a software program to generate random stock numbers for your inventory if you desire. You don't need to do this; you can do it manually it's not that hard. Then I mark the outside of the box with my account such as Bob's discount. It'll be Bob, then a string of numbers for box 1. Like this Bobs-444255645645-1. Then I'll do Bob and a series of random numbers for box 2. Like this Bobs-4234234234234-2. Each item, of course, has a random number, only the Bobs and the -1 are in every stock number.

I store things with my inventory system, and I have separate boxes or bins for storage. I have plastic boxes to organize everything. Initially, I started using banana boxes from the grocery store. You can go to the store and get them or tomato boxes which are also very sturdy. These you can pick up for free at any grocery store, and they're happy to give them to you. This will keep your inventory separate from everything else.

While you have been reading this, I am sure you have thought of many items you can sell. Be creative, everything you find is a saleable item. I am sure you will find someone out there wants it. One day I lost my favorite fishing lure. It was 20 years old, now where can I find one? Amazon! I typed in the name and found five fishing supply closeout stores. I ended up buying three so I would have spares. I have sold so many used items, as they say, one man's trash is another man's treasure. The point here is to look with an open mind. When I started looking, I found more than three boxes of things just lying around that I could sell. I ended up selling most and made over $3500.00. This alone allowed me to make my first purchase from Liquidation.com.

So when you make your first or second search, look for things that have value. Any value will return money to your pocket. But you may be surprised as to what you will find in your search. As I said, I had over $3500.00 in my house just lying around. And I could have had more if I seriously looked. So start here for your first sales to get your feet wet.

This chapter is short but to the point, so move on now to the next chapter!

Chapter 5 List Your First Item

So you found a whole box full of things that you want to list on Amazon. What to do now? LIST THEM!!

So now fire up that computer and log on to Amazon. Hopefully, all will be fine in our test runs. So let's get started.

Go to the Amazon seller page click on sell an item. Then you need to click find an item to sell, type in what you have. If it is an iPhone, then type in the model number. When you do, this many iPhone's will come up. When these items come up, they will already have descriptions and pictures of what people are currently selling. You choose the one that matches yours. If you don't have an exact match, then you'll have to create a new and what you will also need a UPC for that.

I will tell you another trick; Amazon will require you have a UPC or a barcode for your item. If you need that, I can tell you where to get those codes you can buy 100 of them for about seven dollars. That will also be in the appendix at the back of the book. I'll tell you sometime later why you need these. But for right now we're going to assume you have an item that everyone has. That's an old iPhone 2; now you need to list this iPhone. Find the one has the right memory and is the right color looks, and like the one you want to list. Now trust me, if it's not the right color, exactly the right size then someone will leave you negative feedback. Someone will call Amazon and file an A-Z claim. You will lose the money and the item. Also, Amazon will ban you if you do that more than once or twice.

Make sure your item descriptions are exactly what you have exactly if it's not, create a new item. Create your own barcode and use that item. Make sure you understand this. Otherwise, Amazon will cancel your account, and you can't blame anyone but yourself. Follow the procedures, I know it sounds like a lot of work, and it is. But once you get the hang of it, you will do it so quick you won't even think about it. I can go through 40 boxes the size of banana boxes or larger in about a day. This is complete with all kinds stuff pulling out the things I don't need. I will separate the items and then get them all listed. If I can do this in a day, you can too; I'm no special person.

Now you have to list your first item. Go to the Amazon seller page and choose inventory. Then add inventory. It will then ask for a UPC or description. If you have the UPC then great, if not then type in a description, name, or the model number. Then a list of items will come up, choose the EXACT item. List how many you have, list the price, and choose the condition. Then add any description needed. BE EXACT. List the item exactly as you see it. Do not sugarcoat the item description it will come back to bite you. Be accurate, and your customers and your Amazon account will love you. Keep careful attention to the description especially if it is used. If it is new, then you can list it as new. Amazon has several categories of used items, used like new, used very good, used acceptable. Make sure you read the description conditions and grade your item accordingly.

List your item, choose the price you want to sell it for. Then choose to add any personal photos you want to or use a standard photo in your description. Describe the item accurately, if it has a scratch on one side then take a picture and show it. If it has a cracked screen, then describe that it will need a new screen. List how much you want for shipping on the item. Then list the quantity that you have and then choose the price you want to sell it for. There are no negotiations or best offers. You choose the price you want to sell it for.

If you want to get serious about this, I will give you a link at the end of the book for repricing software. This repricing software reprices your items every few minutes to one penny less than the competition. That way you are always on top. If needed, it will also raise your price if someone else raises their price. It's valuable software; I use it on my account. It costs only about $10-$15 a month, but it pays for itself with one sale. You can do this manually, but once you get this system working and you have thousands of items in your account, you can't re-price them by yourself. Even if you want to, you can't it's not possible. I have over 50,000 items on Amazon right now; there's no way I can reprice them manually.

After you have chosen your price, you will also need to put in your stock keeping unit or SKU. As I said, I use Bob plus my string of numbers and what box it goes in to. Again like this Bob-2034422rf-1. That way when an item sells I only have one box to go through. Now, this is my way of doing it. You can choose whatever is best for you, but that's the way I do it. Plus doing it this way you keep your inventory organized. This way you can find the items, trust me it will get difficult and will be painful to find things. You'll be pulling out all your hair to find things. If you see a picture of me, you'll understand why I don't have much hair left. It's because I spent so much from time and effort trying to find all these items that I pulled out all my hair. You don't have to this because I'm telling you how I do it. You can choose how you want to and if you're going to lose your hair that's okay.

Amazon also keeps an excellent inventory. You don't need to keep anything separate, but I like to know what I have in my way, it's my preference. I also keep a running total of the amount of money I have in inventory as well. I also keep an inventory list in an Excel spreadsheet. You could use QuickBooks, or you can use any inventory program you want. I do what I do because I like the way I do it and keep a more accurate listing of what I have.

Now you can sit back and wait for your item to sell or be adventurous and list another item. Find another phone, find a camera, find a piece of software that you have that you don't need anymore. Whatever it is you can start by listing the next item.

To list your second item go through the same procedure as above. Create your price, describe your item and list it. Make sure the pictures are accurate and your description. Choose the right category and sell it.

Now another step in the selling is to check your emails regularly. You may not get emails from Amazon for some reason. So you need to log on and find them online in your Amazon message system. Here you can check to see what items you have sold by checking your messages. Amazon always sends you an email to your registered email address. But what if it gets lost or gets marked as spam?? Amazon is your best source for all that is Amazon. Check your messages on the Amazon website to be safe.

Daily you need to log on to your account and check to make sure that there are no messages from Amazon about your account. It may be something you need to take care of right away. Maybe there is an A-to-Z claim; perhaps a customer sent you a message. If someone has bought something, you need to go to orders and then go to ship orders. Find out if any items have been sold and then clicks the ship item icon. There you can put in the weight. Verify the address is the same then input the weight of the item. Weight the item with the box.

Trust me; if you don't weigh it already packed in the box you may pay too much you, or you may pay too little. If you pay too little, the US post while office will bill your Amazon account for the extra money. You will pay it later at a higher rate than you would get with your Amazon shipping discount. Trust me that has happened to me. I am trying to save you some pain. I had the Postal Inspector call me and ask me why I was shorting the weight. She mentioned it was theft by deception, so I bought a scale that day. Again I am making mistakes for you to prevent problems for you.

Again make sure you weigh the item with all the packing and the box. Be accurate otherwise; you will have problems. Then you will need to print your label. You can use any printer, but once you get to the right point, you will want to use a Zebra 450 printer, which is what I use. You can also use a Dymo printer, they are cheaper, but the labels cost more. By the way, when you use a zebra printer, both FedEx and the UPS will give you labels free. I do ship a lot of things with them, so if you ask they will provide you with free rolls of labels.

Remember now after your first sale to pack everything up carefully. You don't want the item you sold to arrive there damaged. After packing you need to take the items off to USPS, UPS or Fed Ex. After doing this send your customer an email to inform them that their item is on the way. You can do this manually at first, but eventually, you will want it automated. You can find automatic software to do this to tell customers that their item has shipped.

Then send another email once they receive the item. Thank them for their purchase and that you hope they're enjoying their item. Tell them if they have any questions or comments to please call you directly. Make sure put your phone number in the email; also put your phone number in the package when you ship it. Use a small business card or a small piece of paper with your name and your phone number.

Do something so that these people can reach you. You can use any of the phone numbers on TEXT NOW. This is a free service on the iPhone app store or Google Play. Or you can get a separate phone number with a different phone. I have separate phones to make it easy. I run a full-time business on Amazon as well as other things. I have multiple streams of income, and that's what I'm going to try and teach you to do.

This way you can make money when and where you want. No one will be your boss anymore, except maybe your wife and your children. But I think you can work with them, right? And that folks is what this entire book is all about, to make you and your family happy. We have finally gotten there. You are free. Now one or 2 sales will not make your life, but it's a start. Once started and you get the taste in your mouth, if you're like me, you will not stop. Once started this is a lifestyle that you want and more importantly one that you DESERVE!!!!

Chapter 6 Your Own UPC

Sometimes when you go to sell an item, the manufacturer will email you telling you to pull the item. These manufacturers will try to prevent you from selling their items. They will tell you that this is their UPC. I never heard of such a thing; I didn't know a company could own a UPC. That is ridiculous but true. However, I found a source for these UP's and Now I own thousands.

So you may have to be creative about how you list them. You may have to buy your own UPC's if you use your own UPC's you are in the clear Because YOU OWN THAT UPC. The manufacturer can't say you are using our UPC. The caveat is that you must use your description and your pictures. It does require some extra work. But now you can sell this item so you will make money on an item that otherwise you would be prevented to sell.

This is a little known trick. I get people asking me all the time how I can do this? I never told anyone until now. I found this out the hard way. I had boxes of merchandise that I could not sell. I had expensive merchandise that was sitting on a shelf in a warehouse. Then I ran across the UPC store. At least that's what I called it. I put on my UPC on the item and voila it sold.

Now, this is a tedious process. You must go on to Amazon and list a new item. It will be in the normal item listing area, do not make a mistake and choose an existing item. You will need to choose create a NEW item. Choose this item is not in our system. Then you must provide them with every bit of information. YOUR UPC, your description. 3-4 bullet points about the product. The manufacturer, where it is made, Condition, Quantity, Price, etc.

Now you have your own UPC and listing. If someone piggybacks, YOU have the right to tell them to get off your UPC. If not you can report them to Amazon for infringing on YOUR hard work. This is fun, right? Brag to your friends? No, not really. But it is cool. Most people will say you can't do this. But I have, and this teaches you how to do it on your own. Check the back of the book for my list of UPC brokers, and then you are off to the races so the speak.

Chapter 7 Getting Paid The First Time

So you have now sold a few items. Now Amazon wants to pay you. Did you set up your account to be paid? Getting paid the first time as a new seller account is exciting. But have you done everything needed? Amazon holds your money for couple weeks; they want to make sure that there are no complaints. They have no problems with you personally, but I don't blame them. You would do the same thing if you had someone selling stuff under your name.. You would want to hold their money for couple weeks. This way you can make sure that the people got the items exactly as they ordered. After all, you could be a scammer. You could have sent bricks instead of the items ordered. It has happened.

So I understand Amazon absolutely 100 %. Don't be worried when you sell something on Friday and you don't get paid on Saturday for it. It takes a couple of weeks at first, but once Amazon knows you, the payments will arrive every two weeks. You can look at your payment schedule in Amazon seller central. Just click the amount at the top right of the screen and then click the payout schedule when the next page pops up. It will tell you when your next pay schedule is. So when you start a new account, they hold your sales proceeds for two weeks. They don't put money in on Saturday and Sunday. So don't worry you will get paid UNLESS you have problems with Amazon. Just read and follow the recommendations in this book to avoid these problems.

As for your accounts, I recommend Capital One 360. They are an excellent resource for bank accounts. Also, you can have multiple business accounts on Capital One Spark. It is very easy, and you can do it all online. If you want you can even name your accounts to match your various accounts from Amazon, eBay, etc. All you need to worry about is making sure you get your money.

So now if you sold your first item, and this item has been paid for, what do you do with the money? Sit back and decide to what can you do with this money? If you are like me, you will want to buy more things to sell. Because once you sell your first thing, you're ready to buy another batch of inventory. This way you can start the process all over again.

After you make your decision, it is time to get serious. Make some plans, see what has sold, in your inventory.

Chapter 8 Manage Your Amazon Account

Hopefully, you've been successful with the selling of your items. Maybe you are starting to get some feedback from many happy customers. Now what you need to do is duplicate that process and find new items to list. Now I know all of you didn't quit your jobs, at least I hope you didn't, and you still have full-time jobs. But hopefully, you are still dedicated to this project and will push on to succeed. At least that is the ultimate point here. Freedom!!

Now you want to try to find some items to sell that are different so you can expand your marketplace. Let's say you sold pet supplies before and now you want to sell clothing. What do you do now? You go to Liquidation.com, and you buy clothing. Now I tell you Liquidation.com because that's one of the main ones that I have used. I have a source of over 30 wholesale companies from where you can buy inventory.

If you took the gift I offered you at the front of the book, then you know all the sources by now. There's quite a few more depending on where you're located. They may be closer to you to use the Liquidation.com. There is one specific source in California that has prices so ridiculous, that I am surprised they can even stay in business. They must be getting their stock for cheap. But they are too far away for me to go there, it is pick up only, and I can't do that from the east coast of the USA.

Find the new item that you want to sell, and then do your research. Find out what the items will sell for and what kind of profit you can make on the items. Watch a few auctions and find out how much you need to spend to buy the items you want for inventory. Once you've done this multiple times you'll be able to do it so quick you won't even think about it. It will be the way you do business. You will do it automatically, and it becomes second nature. Just like any job, you have ever worked. Like anything you have ever done or have ever been trained for. Consider this you're training; I'm showing you all the cheats to save you time and heartache. I am showing you all the things that I made mistakes on so that you don't have to make the same mistakes. I'm saving you the trouble and expense and the time of experimenting by giving you a hard plan. And how to work with the many different situations that may arise.

Now that you've gone through all the steps and created your new account it's time to make your first purchase. Develop your inventory strategy now on how to market these items. Develop a pricing strategy. When you find something that sells great for you, stop what you're doing and immediately search to buy more. I once bought a box of Calvin Klein jeans in various sizes, for $350.00. After shipping, I paid about $8.00 per item. I sold them for $45.00. After that, I bought three more order of jeans to sell. You must always act fast in situations like this.

Once again, as you list be careful to describe your items EXACTLY as they are. As I advised you earlier, once you start your search, please be accurate. Find the items that come up that exactly match your item; there may be 40 of them that are very close, but only one is exactly the right item. You need to read them carefully and make sure that they are exactly matching. If it is not exact your buyers will tell you that you've made a mistake and leave appropriate feedback. Once you have completed your list and box or boxes of items, you can rest for the day and wait for the inventory to sell.

Now the next thing to do is to start repricing your inventory. You can do this manually if you don't use software, which you probably won't when you're beginning. So you will do manual repricing, by doing it manually you check your items every few hours or as often as you can. The best time to do it if you're doing it manually is around 5 PM or 6 PM so that when people come home, they see your best prices. The next best time is after 10 AM on Saturday and Sunday. The rest of the time, prices can stay pretty much the same. In fact, my software raises the prices 2 to 3 times during the day. I noticed fewer people are price matching during the day, so my software raises the prices to make me more money. You may want to use this after you get serious as it is a time saver and money maker for you. Check my list for the software; it will be in the appendix in the back of the book. And there also are the lists of the other free items, so don't forget to check it out.

Your next task is to follow through with your regular daily tasks. That includes checking email, and check your email BEFORE you ship any items. If you ship first and someone wanted to cancel the item, Amazon will penalize you for this. How do you ask? Well, you shipped the package, and even though you canceled the order, a label was created. Amazon now expects that label or package to arrive at its destination. And it will not ever arrive since it was canceled, but you can't convince a computer this. Therefore you have a package that never arrived, and this looks like a bad mark against you. SO CHECK YOUR

EMAIL FIRST!!! Reply to any and all emails from customers and Amazon.

Next check for any messages or notices from Amazon. This includes restricted item notices and pricing errors. But you may also get notices about your account. So check this next.

Next check your orders, go to the orders tab in sellercentral on Amazon. If you have any orders, they will be here. Choose the first item and then choose the yellow button on the right side to ship that item. Choose the weight of your item with the box and all the packing. Then ship the next item on the list, that is if you have multiple items to ship. Now a new tip, do not drop off the packages at the post office in one of the mailboxes. Get them scanned. I have had so many packages not get scanned but delivered, and then the customer files a claim. Get the item scanned first. This saves you a lot of future trouble.

After delivering your packages and getting them scanned, you can relax. Send the wife or husband a text. Tell them that even though you have been busy all day, you missed them.

Now, what do you do? Go to the next chapter.

Chapter 9 Dealing With The Ridiculous Customer

Now I will tell you how to deal with customers. This is going to be an essential portion of your Amazon training, and it is crucial to your happy life on Amazon. When someone complains, you need to handle it right away to prevent a future problem. If not they will file an A-to-Z claim and chances are Amazon will side against you. Remember Amazon takes care of their customers first. They will agree with you most of the time, but it may take time. Who needs the bother, so fix it before it becomes a problem.

I have filed a couple of A-to-Z claims myself, one where the seller was wrong, but I understood why he was wrong. And I assumed why he did what he did what he did. I can't blame him. Even though it wasn't his fault and I understood his position. However, I still wanted my money back because I didn't think the situation was right. It was the right thing for him to do but he refused to do it. I filed an A-to-Z claim even though I was wrong.

Amazon agreed with me without any question. Five minutes later I got an email saying my claim had been the approved. Keep this in mind; you should deal with your customers first. Make sure they contact you before they contact Amazon. If not then Amazon may make an arbitrary decision without your input.

The way to end this issue is to put a simple piece of paper or business card in your package when you ship your items. On this piece of paper put all your contact information. Thank you for the order., my name is (Use whatever the name is you created on your account), please call me with any problems. I will not rest until we have resolved your issue. Customer service is our motto.

Also when you put this paper in your package give them a link to your store. Tell them to contact you with any questions about the product, how it works, or any problems. If you get anything damaged in shipping, let me know so I can take care of you right away. Also, tell them that it's going to be faster than contacting Amazon. Remind them that Amazon sometimes takes 24 to 48 hours to respond to emails. Tell them you are running this operation all by yourself and you will take care of them personally.

This gives customers confidence and most will NEVER call you. You can use the same phone number you have on your account, or you can go to text free on iPhone and Android. This app gives you free phone numbers that will ring right through to your regular phone. You could also buy a phone like I did that has dual sim cards. With two SIMs in the same phone, you have the best of both worlds; this works great for me. Now you have a way to meet customer needs and satisfy them right upfront before any problems arise. This is my way to solve the problem, but you can make your choice as to what best serves you.

Again these are my suggestions, and they work for me, you may have a better idea if so, by all means, use what works best for you. Whatever you say you want to make it sound like they are your only customer. You've only sold one item in your entire life on Amazon, and it was to this person. And you're going to follow them around until the end of the world to make sure that they're happy.

Chances are they'll never call you. But if someone does have a problem they can reach you. Perhaps something will get misplaced, or something gets left out, or you ship the wrong item. (I have done that myself.) Customers will call you, and then you can rectify the situation. If you don't do this, they will email Amazon and file a complaint or leave you negative feedback.

People are empowered that they can harm you by leaving negative feedback. We have created a vengeful society, with all these online reviews. I've had people go on Yelp and leave my Amazon business a poor review because they can. People these days want to express their view right or wrong. They want people to hear them and see them.

If you don't believe that, go online and read any story on Yahoo or Google. Then go to the bottom of the page and read the comments. Everyone has an opinion, and they will tell everyone else that their view is wrong. People feel very empowered today to do this kind of thing, and sometimes it is for vengeance. So expect you're going to get negative feedbacks. It is a fact of doing business.

However, in my feedback section in a later chapter, I will tell you how to get those feedbacks removed. Question is can get the customer to leave it in the right way so that it is removable.

When a customer emails you answer them immediately. I know I've told you that you only need to answer your emails once a day. But when you're first starting out you need to answer emails all day to make sure that everything is taken care of right away. The moment you send out the package, you email the customer letting them know you shipped their order. Also, give them your contact information again.

Be careful as Amazon will sometimes block telephone numbers. And make sure you tell them to contact you immediately with any problems. That way they reach out to you, and not Amazon. This will save you a lot of trouble. Then after they receive the package email them again. Make sure that everything arrived in good condition. Make sure they are all happy and ask them to please leave you a positive review. Tell them again if they have any questions to please contact you.

Let me point this out to you, and I am sure you do the same thing with your purchases. When you buy something, and you are happy with everything, you most likely go on about your life. And even if you're not, I am sure you will not spend 20 minutes writing a review about how your experience was at the mall. How lousy traffic was getting there how you didn't like the salesperson. Most likely you bought your item you went on about your daily life.

Not with Amazon, everyone wants to tell a story. With some of my feedbacks, they exceed way over what they should be. They will tell you how this happened. How this happened and how it has changed their life. They will tell you how their dog is so happy or how their fish is swimming so actively now. Maybe they will say how their bed sheets feel. Or how they got a new girlfriend because your perfume made them feel better. Or how they feel in the shoes that they bought from you. Their life is so much better now, and you made them feel like an important person. People need to tell you their entire life story when you sell them something. You get the picture right?

The only people who are going to write feedback are going to be the people who weren't happy. And some people you can't please. I've given people things at no cost if it is my error. I will apologize and say that since the item didn't arrive on time, I will provide you with a full refund. And if or when the item arrives you can keep the item.

Now I don't do that with expensive things. But if you think about the cost at which I get things I can do it anyway with no worries. I have told you how much I pay for inventory. I may spend two or three dollars for something even if it's $100 item. Even though it is still only two or three dollars, it is still a mindset. But I have in my head that this thing is worth fifty dollars, and now I'm giving it away. You must do it; this makes most people happy. But some people if you came to their house and committed suicide right in front of them, they would say you didn't do it right. You should do it earlier; something would be wrong.

You can't please everybody, so don't get into the bad feeling and say oh well, I should've done this or maybe this. You can't it won't work and it will frustrate you. Do your best always and try to make sure that you've given the customer all the contact information. And once you've done this for a while, you'll know who the problem people are. You will know them by the areas they live in or by the tones of their emails. Certain countries I do not sell to also, to avoid scams. And If I do sell something there, I take care of them extra special. It only takes you a while to know who they are.

The others that tell you nothing, most likely because they are happy with your product and your services. So email them and ask them to make sure they leave you a good review, tell them you would appreciate it. More positive reviews will way outnumber the negative reviews. If you don't keep ahead of this, your account will get canceled if you have too many negative feedbacks or too many A-Z claims.

If your account gets canceled, I have solutions for you. I will tell you how to work with the A-to-Z claims in a later chapter. I will tell you how to deal with Amazon feedback in a later section also. Contact your customers throughout the process of the sale.

I know I have said email, your customers and you are thinking, wow that's a lot of emails. Well, you can set up automated software to do this to you to send all these emails to you. Amazon will let you know when the item got there. When it does arrive send your buyer a barrage of emails every few days.

After the sale send them an email thanking them for the sale, send the same message after a week or so. Maybe again after a couple of weeks send them an email again about their purchase. I always send 4 to 5 emails to each customer, reminding them again to come back and buy something. I get them from sellers that I buy things from hitting me up for feedback, and I am not upset. Done correctly it is not spamming your customers. But tread lightly to avoid falling into the spam trap.

Give them an offer, so it is not like spam, I will remind them if they buy from you again they will get a 10% discount. That's what Amazon charges you in fees. This is a great a way to make some extra money and build up a steady following on your sales page.

Most the times I'd I don't leave feedback because I don't have time. I never give anybody a negative I'd I don't have the time to be vindictive, I understand things are not perfect. So again, love your customers and send them emails through every step. If you do this your life will be peaceful on Amazon.

We will deal with more feedback tips in the next chapter.

Chapter 10 Inventory

Amazon has an excellent inventory system. However, I have noticed some recurring errors over the years. One issue is things just disappear. No, they are still on my shelf but just not on the Amazon site anymore.

I first noticed it after my second month when I went to pull an item for shipment to a customer. As I pulled that item, I saw something that I expected should have been sold already due to the popularity of the item. I went back to my desk in my garage and checked my inventory, and it was gone. I relisted it, and it sold within hours.

I then decided to recheck all my inventory. I had only three boxes, so it was not much of a challenge. After I completed my check, I found eight items not listed. I relisted them once again and went on my way. And yet three weeks later I checked again, lo and beheld there were five different items not in my inventory.

I did not at that time use any software, just my eyes, hands, and Amazon. But somehow things were disappearing from my online store. So my guess was it was just getting booted off by software, I went back and looked at reports on Amazon, and I could see the inventory, and what days it was there and when it disappeared. I spoke with Amazon with no results.

I finally decided just to check my inventory every day. I opened one box each day to check the contents. This solved my issues. I never found the result or reason as to why this happened. Nor could Amazon explain it to me in a fashion that I understood or believed.

Eventually, I went to a software solution that maintains my inventory on my computer and then pushes it to Amazon daily. This resolved the issue once and for all. However, it is another expense out of my monthly profits.

I put this chapter here only for information so that IF and when this happens you will know why or at least what is happening.

Chapter 11 Feedback Removal Your Worst Enemy

As I told you before people are empowered to express their views about the item that they received. Most people leave product feedback, especially if you coax them into it. If someone starts emailing you, you will soon know they're going to be a pain in the know what. Then you will need to push them in the right direction. You will say yes you understand how bad the product is and you agree with them. And agree that the manufacturer shouldn't be doing that, or the manufacturer should've done this. Make sure you work into whatever it is they're thinking and get on to their side. That way they are not so angry at you. And believe me, people do get mad at you over a five dollar item. They will be screaming and yelling how stupid you are and so ridiculously a loser.

But you know people are empowered behind their computers because they can hide. They would never do that to you in front of you or right in your face. I'm sure you see the same reactions from people on the road. People cut you off and be nasty and honk at you and shake their fist at you. But if you would be standing outside the car or in a line someplace with these same people, this would not happen. No one would ever do that to you because they would be afraid of what you might do. You might turn around and jack their jaws or beat the living you know what out of them.

Most people only have time to make comments about you is if they want to make bad comments. So if you have a good product and you sell a lot of it, you will get good feedback. But any serious comments will be bad ones. These people are empowered, and they believe they can control your destiny. The rest will rarely make good detailed comments about you because they don't have time. I don't have time. I rarely leave feedback on anything I buy. The only time people will leave feedback is when they have something nasty to say. People are vindictive, and now they can sit behind the computer and hide. They can do things that they would never say in front of you right to your face.

People do that on Amazon and on eBay. They do it on every internet site because they feel empowered. As long as they can hide behind their computers, people will do this to you because they can. When you think you're getting a customer like that push them into the fact that the product is terrible. Remember it's not you, not your service it's the product that's bad.

Here is today' big tip. Amazon removes product feedback. Amazon will remove feedback if someone says that the product is bad. Or they say this is bad about the product or that the item doesn't make them happy. Or maybe the way it was designed, the way it looks. Or the way it fits, the color, it doesn't look good on them or the fact that the moon is blue. Whatever they say, as long as its product feedback, Amazon will remove it. All you have to do is ask them; Amazon will help you. Most of the times it's an automatic removal when you click feedback review. Make sure you click that its product feedback.

This is not being dishonest or gaming the system. The customers are gaming the system to get free items. You are protecting yourself. You can't control what people think about the items you sell. This is internet sales, and people have different opinions. Especially since people cannot hold or touch the products, it is understandably difficult. So one may see it a different way than other customers. As long as they are as described, then you are doing nothing wrong. If you sell junk and send the wrong item or broken items, then you DESERVE the bad feedback.

They have some algorithm or scanning software that scans for certain words. When they hit that word they automatically remove it, no questions asked. Nothing you need to do on your part. It's excellent, and on the rare chance that Amazon doesn't exclude the feedback you can email them. Point out the words that make it a review. If you've done your job and coaxed the customer into leaving the proper feedback, it will be gone.

Once you get good at it, you'll know how to do it. Then the feedback will be removed. If it's feedback about the post office about how stupid they were, you can get them to remove that too. That's not you either. That's an item review Amazon will remove it.

Product feedback is what we are concerned with here. If you did you ship it broken then, that's your mistake. That's not product feedback. That's the only feedback Amazon is concerned with and nothing else. When someone leaves feedback like the seller sold me an item and it was broken, it will stay on your account. Unless you get very creative with customer support in your words. It can be done. I have done it many times.

Also, people will leave feedback and say item didn't arrive on time. To get this removed you go in and look when it was supposed to arrive by. Look to see when the item says is supposed to be there. If it says between December 1 and December 14, then that's when Amazon says it supposed to be there. If the item arrived on the 12th and the customer says it arrived late, you can get this removed.

Trust me people will do this because they want a refund. They hope you'll give them a refund. It's a game. You have to play it better than they do. Amazon will say that this is a lie and will again remove the feedback.

So your winning here, all you have to do is coax people into the right way, and you can get feedback removed. Once you get the hang of it, you will get very good at it. You can coax Amazon into doing this for you all the time. Another example, if the buyer says that the seller shipped late but you didn't send it late, then that gets removed.

And another tip is the best time to email for feedback removal is between 930 and 1130 at night Eastern Time. That's one of the best time I have found. This is when the agents switch over from American agents to Indian or Japanese agents. However, they have the Amazon software going and are ready to help. I don't know, but I tend to find out by the names and accents that they are not American.

Sometimes they help because you can push them in the right direction. Or because they don't have a full command of the language. Maybe it's because they are happier to assist you. I find Americans aren't so easy to help us. They will tend to agree with you if you try doing it during the day and if it's a legitimate review of the item they remove it right away. But if it's marginal wait between 930 and 1130 and someone there will help you.

If you don't get the response, you need then open up another case. This time choose other as the need for the case and start all over. I never open up more than one case at a time about the same item. I used to blast them with 3 or 4 cases at a time. But I've had situations where I've opened up two or more cases because I want to bombard them and get them to do what I wanted. Eventually, I would get one who would say yes that is a feedback review and we are going to remove that for you. But then someone else would review it and say, we're sorry, but that doesn't qualify for removal. Then they will go and put it back on my account

I don't know the inside system, but the feedback comes back. Then you have to go back to the first person who emailed you. Tell them, thank you very much for helping me, but that feedback is still there, can you please remove it again? They will do that; they will reply that it was a mistake and error or a glitch. But they will say yes you're right it should be removed, we apologize. We don't know what happened. It's a mistake I learned, so I send one at a time. Bombarding them once worked but now it doesn't. It's changed now; it may work again in the future.

The point here is to be creative with your reasons that it is product feedback. Whatever your goal is, try always to word it so that it looks like product feedback. Even though someone says something about how this or that happened with the item, be creative. And most feedback can be removed. Remember it is still removable on many fronts. Look at your options. If there's something, Amazon can do they will help you. Most people leave feedback and then never go back to see if it is still there. They feel great they left it, and you feel even better since you had it removed. All parties involved are happy.

If you look at any feedback, anyone leaves you can see what I mean most of it is removable. Go to Amazon right now find any seller, you want and look at their feedback. See what it says about them, about the item or the sale. Anything that someone says, you can look at it with your new found eyes and say that's a review of the product. Since it's a review of the product, it gets removed. I'm sure you can look at it and see how things can be twisted with your own mind. All you have to do if it doesn't say the magic words is to get the creative hat on. If it doesn't say, those magic words get creative. Whatever those magic words are that Amazon needs I wouldn't know for sure, they seem to change all the time. If it doesn't say what it needs to say, then you need to be able to twist it into your way. You need to make sure that Amazon sees the idea that it's a review of the item.

Like I said look at any seller even Amazon, and you'll see what I mean. You can get most feedback removed. If you go to my Amazon account, you would see that I have over 9000 positive feedbacks. Out of that, I have only 12 that are negative. I've had my account canceled because of negative feedback. Once I went in and got them to remove the bad feedback my account was reinstated.

Also, you can appeal to a customer to get the feedback removed if you think isn't justified. Even if you think you should have done something different or you know you were wrong. A lot of people are reasonable ordinary people as you know. I know I said you can't please everyone. But most of the people will remove the feedback if you make a genuine effort to console them.

Be sincere when you say, sorry for the delay in shipping on your item. Tell them that you can't understand what happened, but you will do whatever is needed to fix the issue. Show them that you shipped it on time, they can see the tracking, but the post office must have delayed the delivery. And even though it's not my fault, I accept full responsibility. But because it was the post office and not me, I would appreciate if you would remove the feedback. They will do this most of the time.

If they don't know how to do it tell them to reply that they would like the feedback removed in an email. That's good enough; you can show that to Amazon. Then they will remove that feedback for you with no questions asked.

Now I can't tell you the exact words to say to Amazon. Because I don't know what feedback you're going to get but I'll give you an example here. One of my feedbacks that I had removed said that item arrived but is made of poor quality material. They said when they looked through the glasses, it looked like they were looking through an old barn window. Now unless you manufacture the glasses, you're not responsible for that feedback. That's a product review; chances are Amazon will remove it right away. If they don't, you email Amazon and say this is a product review. Remind them that you are not the manufacturer of these glasses. Therefore that is a review of the product and not my services. Even if the buyer said this seller was terrible, the seller sold me this junk or I don't like him. As long as the words are in there that this item looks like it is made from glass from an old barn, then that's not you.

You didn't make the item, all you did was sell the item, someone else in some other place else made the product. Unless you are the manufacturer of the items, you are selling on Amazon you are safe. Even then it's still a product review it's not you are not your services and Amazon will again remove the feedback. Most people don't know this. This is an inside tip for you. This is something that is going to save you a lot of time and save you lot of money and a lot of worries. You'll have more hair than I do, this is what happened to me I pulled out all my hair because I was angry and frustrated.

The one thing I will tell you about selling on Amazon is that Amazon people will irritate you. In all internet sales, people will annoy you to the point that you want to scream, but the beautiful thing is it's only momentarily. That person may irritate you so bad, but chances are you'll never see or hear from them again. All you have to do is walk away from the computer, and they're gone, it's done. It's not like retail sales where someone stays there and bugs the heck out of you, and you can't escape. You can choose to ignore their emails and mark them as no answer required. Move on with your business and happy life. See you later buddy; they can scream and yell and do whatever they want. It's all okay. You can smile all day now.

So, follow these procedures, and you'll get 90% of your feedback removed. If you have feedback that you receive that you can't that you tried once or twice and you can't get it removed then email me. I'll try to work out a good presentation for you to present Amazon so they can get the feedback removed. Don't try 50 times because eventually they'll lock you out and say they're not interested. You can email me for help.

There are people out there who will charge you 10 or $20 for this service. Quite honestly, it's worth it because your feedback is your reputation. They will guarantee they will get removed because they're better at it than I am, and I've actually used them once before. One time that I couldn't get feedback removed I had to ask for help. Whatever they said they never told me because I had to let them have access to my account which was scary. But they took access to my account and went about to call Amazon. They pleaded my case and boom the feedback was removed. They didn't send it to my messages because I would've been able to see it what was said. Then I would tell you what they how they did it. I have no idea, but the feedback was removed that was all that really matters. It might be that they knew someone on the inside. They might have called to say remove this for me, and I will give you five bucks. I have no idea but it but it worked.

Bottom line here and it is probably needless to say, follow the procedures here that I have listed. If you have a question or you have a problem, or you can get something removed then email me. I'll help you out for free to the best of my abilities. If that doesn't work and it bothers you, then you can always try one of these services, and I will list them at the end of the book.

Chapter 12 A-to-z Claims

A-to-Z claims are your worst nightmare. They stay on your account for 30 to 90 days, and they can affect you and get your selling privileges removed. Amazon will tell you that your account is going to be suspended because you have a high A-to-Z rate. And there is nothing you can do, well at least at the beginning of this process. I will tell you how to appeal those later in this chapter. I will even help you write a letter if necessary to get it removed. Even if you're not at fault Amazon will still remove your selling privileges. Remember they need to protect their customers from bad sellers. So do not take it personally, you would do the same thing if you were in their shoes.

There are ways to mitigate this if your account is in jeopardy. One is to reach out to the customers and offer to resolve the issue if they close the A-Z claim. Then of course then it is not counted against you. This will work, but you should have already done this earlier in the process. The other is to win the claim. If you win the claim, the A-Z is not counted against you.

The A-to-Z rate dramatically affects your Amazon account. It's called the ODR, or order defect rate. Negative feedback also counts towards the ODR. With a high ODR rate, you will be warned, or you suspended. A-to-Z claims are kind of hard to defend against, but they can be done.

When you get an A-to-Z claim, don't answer right away. That's the worst thing you can do because you're angry or upset because you think your customer is a moron. Most of them are of course, but that is beside the point. People sometimes don't understand things, and it is easier to complain and get free items. After they complain, Amazon will refund them, and THEY KEEP the item. It's a WIN WIN yes??

When people file A-to-Z claims, they want the item for free typically. But not always, sometimes it is a misunderstanding. Maybe they don't know how to use the item. Perhaps you can educate them on its use. Even though any retail store would never offer this service, people think that with internet sales you MUST help them.

One of my best claims was a lady bought a heated winter ski jacket about five years ago. The description of the jacket shows that it is the jacket only. On the very bottom of the page, it shows you that accessories needed for this jacket. Which include heating elements, the battery pack, a controller, a charger. The customer spent $199 for the jacket. The customer emailed me and said where are the controller and the battery pack? I need to have these for this thing to work. I replied that they were not included. She said it's not a proper jacket if it's not included. I responded again; please reread the ad, this item is not included in the sale. I even wrote a note in the description that said, please note as per the manufacturer this item is ONLY the jacket. Any other needed accessories are purchased separately.

These items were not included because you can buy larger battery packs. You can also buy faster chargers, and you can buy heavier heating elements to meet your needs. These items are not included and must be purchased separately. The lady still didn't see it that way. And after two or three days of going back and forth, I contacted Amazon. I explained that this customer is trying to extort me for extra items not included in the sale. I told them she was threatening to leave back feedback unless I give her what she wants. They said don't worry but, she did anyway. She left me a negative review and then she filed an A-to-Z claim. I was able to get the feedback removed because it was a review of the item. I pointed out that the item does not include these things. And the customer wants items that were not included in the original sale. Amazon removed the feedback. Now the A-to-Z claim was another problem. I thought about it for more than 24 hours, and then I worded my reply as follows.

"Customer purchased this item on March 4, 2011. This item was described as being a heated ski jacket. According to the manufacturer's description, it states these items are not included. It even says at the bottom of the ad that there are accessories needed to complete this purchase. Those accessories might include a battery pack, a controller, heating elements and a charger. This customer is demanding that I provide her with the controller so that she can operate the item. This means she most likely already has heating elements and a charger. She also wants a battery pack as well. Maybe because hers is broken or because he has these already, I don't know her buying history. I know that these items are not included. I also know that as soon as I provide her with one of these items, she will want another item."

"These items are not included even on the manufacturer's website. And it states this in Amazon's description of the item. It states that these items are not included. This is a bogus attempt for items and services not included in the sale and an obvious extortion attempt. This is a violation of Amazon policies at the best and criminal at the worst; please do not allow this to continue. Please do not grant this A-to-Z claim. This is a fraudulent attempt to obtain items through extortion."

Amazon reviewed the claim and denied it. The customer then filed a chargeback. I used the same wording to defend that as well. Amazon used that to deny the claim. The chargeback since it was won did not affect my ODR my order defect rate. If someone leaves you negative feedback and files an A-to-Z claim only one will count against you. If you get the A-to-Z claim back removed, but not the feedback, you will still have one hit against your ODR. If you get the feedback removed but the A-to-Z claims stay, you still have one mark against your order defect rate. You need to get both removed to clear your name.

Sometimes Amazon will review a claim and decide that the customer is wrong. But they're going to grant the claim because they want happy customers. They will allow their claim but not take the money from your account. Amazon will grant their claim and give them a refund. That claim is a win for you because it says claim granted but Amazon funded. The seller is not at fault. So Amazon gives the money from their account, and you don't get charged with the A-to-Z claim. You're only charged for the A-to-Z claims if Amazon grants it, and it says seller-funded. That hits your ODR and hurts you financially.

If you have too many A-to-Z claims rates and too many negative feedbacks, this will affect your ODR. This will result in your account being terminated. It's a simple matter-of-fact, so keep your nose clean and try to do everything you can to limit these. If you email me, I will send you one of my favorite excuses for A-to-Z claims to get out of them. You can change the wording to match the product that the customer is complaining about. And most A-to-Z claims unless you didn't respond to the customer can be resolved.

That is unless you ship them a rock and they were supposed to receive a $2000 radio. Or you send them a blue coat, and they wanted a green coat. Most of these claims can be resolved quickly if you try. It was a mistake, and you can take care of it and send you out the item and keep Amazon informed so they can see the progress. That way Amazon will know that you were trying to work with the customer. They will close the A-to-Z claim in your favor and tell the customer why they made their decision.

Amazon is a very customer-centric organization. They will try to make sure the customer is taken care of most of the time at the seller's expense. They don't care so much about hurting you as they do about helping the customer I've seen this on my own. I have seen this when I have bought things myself. So your best bet is to try and make the customer happy. Try to make sure that Amazon can see that you've done everything to make the customer happy. It is the customer that is unreasonable. Word your sentences and your responses very carefully. Make sure you always put your contact information in and then reply the A-to-Z claims. Again do this late at night, these are the people you want to review your appeal. They will evaluate your claim, and they will see that you been trying to help the customer. Hopefully, they will deny the claim.

Again, don't reply right away and be careful to write your responses very accurately. You need always to make your point in the first 3-4 sentences. Otherwise, the rep will deny the claim they do not have time to read your long drawn out story. If you make your point up front, you have caught the reps attention and then get you an explanation in detail. Take a look at my response. I pointed out the customer bought only the jacket and that Amazons' description says precisely what I have been explaining to the customer. Now that I have their attention, I can go into detail. Remember Amazon has MILLIONS of buyers and sellers, so they need to resolve issues as quickly as possible. Sometimes this is a benefit to you if you make our point strong. They will stop and decided in your favor. If not they will deny the claim. But you can appeal that and then you must again make a strong 3 -4 line point. Appeals work only 20-25% of the time so do your best work first.

If you have an issue, send me a message, and I will help you at no cost to you at all. I will do my best.

Chapter 13 Responding To Emails

Amazon has multiple metrics on which they base your performance. Like how fast you responded to an email, or if you ever answered. If you wait longer than 24 hours that's hit on your account; they will tell you that you were late and of course that's a bad thing. You need to respond as fast as possible to Amazon even if it's once a day, as I have suggested doing.

Be sure you follow the same procedure and you it once a day. That still falls within 24 hours. My account has an autoresponder. My largest account on Amazon responds to the customer automatically. The email tells them that I will contact them within 24 hours. But if they have any questions that need immediate care to please call us at blah blah blah number. Amazon picks that up as a response within 24 hours, so I never get a late response message mark on my account.

However, when I first started out, it was hit or miss. Sometimes it worked well and other times not so well. Then it worked fine after I changed a few words in the message. You could use the autoresponder and maybe it will work for you. If not then tinker with it. If you play with it, you may get it to pass the Amazon messages requirement. I would give you my words exactly, but it changes so often it would be of no use to you. I will give you an example in the next paragraph. I can't guarantee for sure what's going to happen. Its trial and error with this may work or it may not.

"Thank you for contacting us here at Central USA Liquidators. Due to the high volume of emails, it may take us up to 24 hours to respond. We need rest too, especially on weekends! Please call us at 555-555-5555 if you have an immediate issue that can't wait. Thank you, and we look forward to serving you.

Ryan"

Amazon also tracks if you responded to the customer and resolved their issue. Amazon will also track if you ship the item late. Items must be shipped when they are supposed to be sent and no later than it's supposed to. If you ship too late, it will cost you and Amazon will penalize you. Your best bet is when an order comes in you ship the same day. If it's on the weekend, you can wait to Monday. What I do to prevent this metric from hurting me is to log into my computer from home. I ship the item; I print postage, I put a packing slip on the back of the label to help me find it the next day. Now it's shipped on the same day that the order came in. Everything is now shipped promptly. Now if there is a computer failure or there's a power outage, you are still saved.

Amazon doesn't care if you lost your Internet for whatever reason. Maybe you didn't pay your bill, or you have sloppy service. Amazon doesn't care; it's your responsibility to get items shipped on time. So if I need to drive to someplace and use a public computer, I will. I would recommend, or you take your computer to a coffee shop and use their Internet. If you do that you can save the labels and the packing slips as PDF files. Then when you get to a printer either at home or the office, you can print them with ease. Amazon only cares that you did your job and did it in the allotted time frame.

After all, Amazon did do the hard work; they found the buyer. Now it is all in your hands so do your job right too. Amazon, your customers, and your BANK ACCOUNT will love you.

I will tell you that if Amazon sees too many late shipments will warn you first then suspend your account. You need to make sure that you stay on top of this. But again, once you start doing this, it will be an automatic task. You won't even think about it, and your account will be in excellent shape. But if you make a mistake and you will get your account suspended for poor performance. I will tell you and give you some samples in the appendix, in the back of the book which I will send to you free. These will help you to get your account reinstated due to poor performance.

Amazon tracks multiple things that can affect you and you need to stay on top of them every day. Make sure when you log into your account before you ship any items you check your Amazon emails. You may receive an email from a customer saying, please cancel this item I don't want it now. If you don't do this first and you have already created a label, it will affect your account. You will have affected your package didn't arrive within the allotted time metric. Now don't worry you can go in and cancel your label to get your money back, so you are safe there. The customer is happy that you canceled their order and they got their money back. However, Amazon still tracks the shipping label.

When that label or package does not get delivered, Amazon counts this as a failure. And of course you never shipped the item, because the customer asked to cancel it, so you have now created a problem. Amazon tracks that you sent 100 packages but three of them didn't get to the customer. These were your canceled orders.

Your shipping rate is now under 97%. Amazon has a limit of 96%. You can only have 4% your packages not arrive on time otherwise. Amazon will penalize you. Amazon can then suspend your account because your shipping is not accurate enough. The item didn't get to the customer on because you never shipped the item. Remember the customer canceled it and you can't ship an item that was never paid for. But Amazon will not listen to this, and they shouldn't have you.

You need to make your process better. Therefore you need to go in each day, check your emails first. Trust me I have made this mistake more than once, making sure there are no cancel requests. If so cancel those first then Amazon will not penalize you for that, and then you're good to go. If you don't do this, you may ship enough items, and this will not affect you. However, if you ship only three or four items a week, it will affect you. Amazon only sees that one or two of the items never got there. They will email you telling you that your arrival rate is too low. Yes, you can appeal this too, and it will sometimes get removed. But why bother to do it right the first time and save you problems.

They will warn you that you should use the proper procedure, which is what I am teaching you here. And that procedure is to check your email to be sure that there are no cancels. These cancel again will not affect you if the customer asked for it. But they do affect you if you ship the item, then it never arrives. So if you do it right, you have no worries.

Chapter 14 The Set Up

You will find some time that returns or requests for returns are a setup. If another seller sees that you're selling their products for less than what they are selling it for, they can buy your product so they can leave you and negative feedback. They are sellers as well, so they know exactly how to word the feedback so it can't be removed. They will use an account that can't be traced back to them. So it's no use to complain. But you know exactly who did this You will get an email saying the bottom price for this item is $110.24. You may not sell it for less than this to doing so violates the policies of their company.

I sold a clock onetime for less than the minimum price; I was selling it for $94. Nothing wrong with it the item was brand-new, I bought it myself and never used it. I wanted to undercut everybody by ten bucks. I sold the item quickly; the thing was I sold it to the company that makes them. They then left me negative feedback. Why because they didn't want me selling the item lowers than the MINIMUM price. When I responded to them that this is the private sale and I want to sell the clock at any price I wanted. I added that you have no control over my price. This is America;

we have a free economy. They never responded, they just bought the item and then left me negative feedback after buying it. I could not get that feedback removed because it was carefully worded

However, vengeance was mine. I did the same thing to them later. Very vengeful of me I know it is something I shouldn't have done. I no longer do this for fear of karma, that it will bite me back later. But you could go to a computer library if you knew who it was for sure and buy something from them, then leave them negative feedback. You can give a bogus address say it never got there and then you get your refund. That is if you want to do that, but remember what I said, it will always bite you back. I'm sure the people got their karma for doing what they did to me. So the better solution is when someone makes a complaint like that to pull the item right away.

Then a week or 2 later put it back on at such a low price that someone will snap it up right away. This clock was $108 on everybody else's account I had mine priced at $94. I thought that was good enough but apparently not it was there for a couple of days. I want it gone right away so with another item I reduced it down very low. I will use a clock as an example; I would reduce it down to $75. Remember I am only paying 3 or 4 dollars for these items anyway including shipping.

So it's not hurting me all yes I lose 10-20 bucks but don't be greedy. I sold the thing within an hour. The seller never had a chance to email me. I never got an email from them saying hey you're selling our item too cheap and didn't have to argue with them. This company could have hundreds of employees. Maybe thousands of employees; all they have to do is ask someone to buy the item and then leave negative feedback. You can't fight that, your best idea is to either mark it back up to the price they suggest. Then sell it on another website at a low price before they get a chance to see it. Or pull it off and not worry about it because these companies will do this eventually. And you cannot convince Amazon of this, you can only suspect that happened, but you can never prove it.

Amazon is right; you can never prove it. They are very good at leaving the feedback so that it's a problem with you and not the item. They are very careful with the feedback and the way it was worded it was and what happened was your fault, not the item.

Again, as I said, people feel empowered these days to try to control your destiny by leaving you feedback. You need to control your destiny by making sure they don't have the opportunity to do so. Make sure you do everything right to prevent this. And if they do have a problem, goad them or push them into leaving feedback that is a review of the item. But not for you and your services. Their review can and will be removed. They feel good because they left you bad feedback. Chances are they will not come back and look at your account to see the feedback; most aren't that spiteful. Even if they do nothing can be done its gone, and Amazon's word is final. They'll leave you their feedback and move on with their poor life and live with a warm and happy fuzzy feeling.

Now you can go on about your life because you got the feedback removed and they'll never know about it. They don't get an email saying; hey we removed the feedback because we thought you were an idiot. If they did, then they would tell them what you left a feedback review, and it's not allowed. People would get smart eventually and start leaving feedback about you personally. This is feedback that you will not get removed. So it's good they go on about their lives. You're happy, they are happy, and Amazon is happy. By the way, only the last two are really important.

So don't fall into this trap of leaving vengeful feedback. It will come back to haunt you. If they figure out it was you and they can somehow link it you, Amazon will cancel your account. And even if they can't prove it, they'll go along and have their uncles or aunts buy something to leave you more feedback. Then you get your account canceled. Yes, I know this has happened. One guy even called me and told me he was going to do it. He said I'll make sure you never sell on Amazon again; you 're an asshole.

I don't know what I did that irritated him so much, he never told me what it was. In 2 weeks he bought 18 items and left nine feedbacks all negative. All the feedback was over stupid stuff and all over three dollar items. I spent weeks suspended and tried to convince Amazon it was the same person. Somehow Amazon linked the accounts and suspended them all. They reinstated my account right away. They figured it out that these negative feedbacks were from the same person. After I complained, I received a call from Amazon apologizing for this. And they blocked these buyers forever. And then it never happened. I have had no negative feedback in over two years.

Later I received an email from this man telling me he was back on Amazon again; he warned me would be after again. I thanked him for the warning. I had my lawyer send him a letter. It advised him that with the evidence from Amazon and the emails sent to me he would file criminal charges. He stopped right away. It was all fun and games until I stood him up. I dropped it and never reported him to Amazon. I'm a better man than he was and went on with life. I have a feeling like this; now I know you're an idiot and you know you're an idiot. We both agree on something and let's move on with life. So that's where I left it.

So keep in mind that there are people like this. Do what you can to avoid and ignore them. I am telling you this story, so YOU don't make the same mistakes I did and get caught up in the loop. If you find yourself in a situation like this, slow down and calmly think about your actions or just move on and forget about it. Stupid people will eventually lose interest. And you will be a better person for ignoring them.

Chapter 15 Broken Items Scam

Have you been scammed by a customer claiming they received a broken or different item? After you have been selling for a while, you'll see this happen. You will get an email saying the item I received was broken and doesn't work. You will know by the tone of their email; they want the item for free. Yes, you can figure this out by listening to the way they're saying it. The first clue is when you offer to replace the item they say no. They reply that they want a refund.

Well, if the item is defective and you wanted in the first place, wouldn't you want to have a replacement? Now you would again have what you wanted, a brand-new item? Now that only makes sense. At first, you feel bad for them, and you give them a refund. Then you start understanding that this was a scam to get free items. Amazon is so good about the fact that if you order something and you tell them is defective, they will send you out a new one. And a lot of times they will not ask for the item back. They may even give you a refund because they don't have any more in stock and you get to keep the item. Some people have gotten very used to this.

So people will tell you that the item is broken hoping to get it for free. The first thing I offer is a replacement. But when they tell me that they don't want a replacement only their money back, I know this is a scam. Since I know, it's a scam I provide them with the shipping label and say, please return the item for full refund. Amazon requires them to return the item once you request them to return the item. This is a secret trick. Most times they will tell me I threw the item away just give me a refund, and we'll call it even. Or something along those lines, you know the routine. I will say no, Amazon requires the item be returned. I am sorry this is as per Amazon policy unless I have instructed you to throw the item away, you must return it before you get a refund.

Now I have them. They've already told me they don't have the item anymore; they threw it away. So now they go and file an A-to-Z claim on Amazon. I tell them again, please return the item, but they won't return the item because they want to keep it. They want a refund and to keep the item. Amazon will also tell them that they must return the item for a refund. The seller has provided you with a label, please use that label within ten days and we will track the item. Amazon is now on your side. If the item is not returned, then Amazon will close the claim against them and in your favor. Sometimes I've gotten so bold as even to provide them a prepaid label to force the issue. I know I don't have to, but I want to prove a point. But more often to be nice to prevent negative feedback.

Niceness sometimes gets you. Don't be nice. Don't be like me. I learned my lesson. Don't send them a label. Tell them if the item is genuinely defective, to just return the item. Once you receive it and verify that is defective, you will send them a refund. They will file a claim with Amazon. Amazon will tell them the same thing and might even grant the claim but not hold you responsible. This is good for you and customer wins, but they still cheated you. However, you didn't get hurt by the claim. Or Amazon will tell them exactly what you've said to them, please return the item, and the seller will issue a refund.

Now some people are so bold and will send an empty box back to you. When this happens, I report this Amazon. I also tell the customer when I received the empty box I had it opened by a US postal employee. I inform them that mail fraud is a felony offense. I will have USPS proceed with the investigation unless you drop the claim with Amazon. Now keep in mind I didn't do this, but I have made friends with several great postal employees. On occasion, I ask them to call a customer on my behalf. Shortly after that, they close the claim. They will close the claim because they know they committed fraud. And they don't want to go further, and they don't want their Amazon account closed. If you get your Amazon account closed, you lose everything you had. All the movies you bought, all your points you had and all your Kindle books are all gone. People don't want that to happen.

People also try the return scam by returning a different item. They will order a watch from you, they will return a watch, but it's a broken one. It's the same one; they will tell you that it's yours and it's broken, they want to refund. But you can see that it's filthy and that it's old. I usually respond, thank you for returning the item. However, you must've made a mistake our items are marked with a dye which can only be seen under a special scope. I usually make it up as I go, I don't do this, but people do believe me. I tell them when I examined this I can see there is no mark on this item. Therefore you must have returned the wrong item by accident. I am returning this item to you so that you may return our item. Thank you very much.

Chances are they will drop their claim, and that's the end of it. If they file a complaint with Amazon, we use the fact that we take a picture of an item that we have and we secure marks on our items. We show how that is visible under a light. Then we show the item that the item they returned has with no mark, and we tell Amazon this is a fraudulent claim. It was evident to us that someone is trying to steal from us.

Nine out of ten times, you will get someone on Amazon who is smart, and they will resolve the claim in your favor. Occasionally, we lose. But you know that that's the game. You can't win all the time we try to win as much as we can. It's a game with some people, but really it is plain and pure theft. People will try to do it, so your best bet is to try to catch these instances and deal with them right away. Deal with them appropriately and try not to get caught up in it. Don't get angry. Unfortunately, this is the nature of the business on the Internet. People will try to scam you always. Amazon has gotten so good at giving people refunds because they want everyone to be happy and people expect it now. And now they expect it from you as well, and they will try to push you into it. Be strong!!

So many times I have called up Amazon because I had a problem with something, all I wanted was a replacement. Amazon will offer to send me a replacement and give me a partial refund. I bought a bicycle that when arrived I found it was damaged. The fender was pushed in, and one of the spokes was bent. This was a very expensive bike and had only had six spokes. It appeared the fender had fallen and pushed against the spoke twisting it. It was a small repair, at the bike shop, around $100. I had hoped they would send me a new bike or give me a little discount.

I took some touch up paint, and I straightened up the fender. I had the spoke fixed at the shop. Most bikes will get bent in the first couple times when you ride it, and it falls over. But no Amazon decides even though it's $1000 bike, to give me a $300 refund. It's not what I asked for, and I said that's not necessary. The lady said no problem; we want to take care of our customers and make sure you're happy. Are you satisfied sir with the way this resolved and I said yes I am. But I said it was unnecessary; you could send me a new bike if you want to? She said shipping is too much to send a new bike; we will do this and make sure you're a happy camper.

I was happy. I ended up buying another bike for myself with the money left after the repair. But guess what? That bike also arrived with a scratch and a dented fender. It must be a shipping thing, so I called them up again. I said look I said I already ordered one bike and it came damaged and now the second bike is also damaged. They still gave me credit on the bike for the damage. This time, however, the wheel was bent more than I expected and it cost me $300 to fix it.

So again to go over the facts again. When you feel someone starting to scam you try to get them to send the item back. If they refuse to send the item back, stand them up. Don't be afraid to do this, you may lose your account, but you can always create a new account. Stand them up and tell them to return the item for a refund. Amazon will agree with you and tell them also to return the item. Or they'll give them their money back and then you'll not be charged with the A-Z claim.

If you feel that someone's returning the wrong item, I recommend to stand them up. Especially if you know the item left without a chip in it, without a break in it and you see that they want a refund. They want to keep the item, or they've exchanged with their broken POS then stand them up. Tell them this is not my item we mark everything with a dye, and this dye can only be seen under a unique light. We would like to return this item to you so that you can send us our item back. Once we receive OUR item back, we will be happy to give you a refund. Ask them if they want their defective item returned to them.

Tell them the serial numbers don't match or whatever you want to say. Most people don't know that there are serial numbers on a watch. They are there, but they're tiny. People know they are on motherboards and computers, things like that so they won't try those. But some will because they are not that bright, stand them up again.

Remember you have to think about your account. If it is such an OBVIOUS scam, Amazon will see it also then you will be safe. Try to work with the customer. You will see who is who after a few sales and you will learn who to stand up and who are making real complaints.

Chapter 16 Shipping

When you ship things on Amazon, you need to make sure you get the weight right. If you pay too much, you wasted money. If you pay too little the U.S. Postal Service will find out when they weigh the packages. If they think it weighs too much, then they will send Amazon a bill. USPS will charge you at the full rate, not your discounted Amazon rate. I did mention this earlier, but it goes to say again buy a good scale weigh things after you have packed them.

I buy plastic shipping bags and ship most everything in these bags. I also get padded envelopes from the U.S. Postal Service. You can go to their website and buy supplies. You can get padded envelopes from FedEx and UPS. I try to fit as much as I can into pre-paid labeled rates like with USPS. I will shove a pair of pants into one of those plastic envelopes, and that protects it from damage. That's less than six bucks a ship 2-3 pounds. Shipping three pounds to California will cost you ten dollars.

However, if you shove those pants into one of those priority mail rate bags, you can save four bucks. You have to look at all your options and think about what's the best way to ship your item and the most cost-effective. Usually, Amazon gives you a list of options from which to choose. There are various rates and carriers to choose from; the prices do vary so remember to choose wisely.

Also when shipping, you need to make sure you use appropriate packing again. I use the padded envelopes from USPS, FedEx or you can buy packing bubble to make sure that's appropriately packed. A lot of times I will ship only an item only in half of a USPS envelope, and this still gets a flat rate. I will save the rest of that envelope for shipping again or for wrapping a package in it. I may even use it as packing, make sure that it's sealed and protected properly. A lot of times when I get orders in from Liquidation.com they come with bubble wrap or they come with paper packing. I save all those, and I use that to ship items to my customers. I save a lot on shipping by recycling.

I used to reuse boxes when shipping to save money, but that can create an issue for some customers. The one problem I have had when using shipping package again is that I've had customers file an A-Z claim. They file a claim that they ordered a mixer and the box on the outside says that it's a water filter system. I reused a box to ship something heavier and protected it inside another box. I usually respond very nicely, please open the box. I tell them that to save both of us time money, that I may have used a recycled box. I tell them that I hope this didn't offend them. I say to them to open the box and inside that box is the item you ordered. I also say that by using recycled boxes I can have lower prices. And of course it's good for the environment by making less waste in our landfill.

People usually respond oh, I'm so sorry you're right. Thank you for saving our environment, and that ends the conversation. So pack well, weigh your package and use the appropriate amount of postage. Make sure it is not too little but not too much, this saves money for you. And it makes sure that it gets there in the right amount of time.

Now shipping to foreign countries, I don't sell the foreign countries. If you're in a foreign country and you are reading this book, and you want to sell to the United States that's all up to you. If you want to sell and you're in Europe, then that's all good. I find it too much of a hassle. I seem never to be able to get the shipping right when I sell, and returns are nearly impossible. I always try to be gentle and not charge the customer too much for shipping. However, for some reason, I end up spending my own money for shipping when the customer should've paid for that.

For example, I'll ship something to Canada. Canada's only couple hundred miles from me. It's not that big of a thing, but it's because going across the border it costs extra money. UPS, USPS, and FedEx all want more money because they have additional procedures that they have to go through. The bottom line is, it costs me more money. I will think that it's only six ounces, six ounces here in this country is just three dollars or less to ship. However, going to Canada that six ounces cost about $10 more. Therefore, if I charge the customer only for five bucks and it costs more, then end up having to pay the extra costs. This eats into my profits.

So be careful when shipping out of the country. If you decide to do so, do your research extensively. I have Mexico, and Canada cut off in my store. Occasionally people will ask me if I will ship something to them and I will tell them, yes, but let me get the rates. I take their information down, and I find out what the exact price is. I ask them to go ahead and buy the item after I have adjusted that item for shipping. This makes excellent customer service and makes all parties involved happy.

So to reiterate, pack your item well, then weigh the item. Use the appropriate packing and envelopes for how you are shipping the item. As in Priority Mail, flat rate, regular mail or for using UPS/FedEx. Look at the prices on Amazon; you'll find that they vary differently. Sometimes I can ship a package for $10 with USPS when it cost me $15 for UPS. Sometimes I can send a package with UPS and FedEx for $7 or $8 when it cost me $20 on United States Postal Service.

So think about what you're doing and use it appropriately. Don't grab the first box you see. Don't do this blindly, look at the rates and you will see that they are very different. Eventually, you will know what cities after a while get better rates and who provides the best service. Do your research. This is all about research, and yes this changes from time to time, so keep up with the rates and save yourself money. It's entirely fine and perfect this week and next week, but it may change in two weeks. It may change in three weeks. It may not change. Just check always to make sure.

Always be diligent and remember you're responsible for your destiny. Now, no one is sitting back to tell you that hey Bruce, you did wrong here, this is what you should do. You're the only one saying that and the only person's going to get hurt is you. Because you're going to lose money, think for yourself. This is what this book is all about reminding you to think for yourself. Becoming your own master and not being a slave to anyone.

Chapter 17 Your First Wholesale Shipment

Now I'm assuming you're ordering from Liquidation.com. If you are ordering from someone else, the same thing will apply. I'm using Liquidation.com her as I said for simple comparison. If you are using someone else, you can substitute the name of your company that you're using.

When you order from Liquidation.com, you will need to have your order sent by UPS if you want it to arrive quickly. If you order by freight, it may take a week or so for them to get out and then 2-3 days for it to be delivered. You could be waiting for several weeks for inventory to arrive. However, the difference is the shipping is super cheap if you order in bulk.

So keep this in mind that your first order should probably be a single order from Liquidation.com. This way it will arrive promptly. Then afterward you can order and plan accordingly. If you watch the auctions over the weekend and you win one, chances are it can ship by Monday or Tuesday. This means you should get your order by the end of the week. That being the case, you can get your inventory out on Amazon, in time for the weekend where you get most of your sales.

When you get your shipment from Liquidation.com, don't go all wild when opening up the boxes. Liquidation.com gives you a list of everything is supposed to be in the box. I do a copy and paste from the website and paste that list into an Excel spreadsheet. It may take you a couple of times to get it right so that it fills up the spreadsheet correctly and doesn't make one big column. Unless you're better than I am. I don't know why it happens, but it does to me all the time. But after I do it a couple of times, it will fill up each section appropriately. Then you can delete the pieces you don't need by going to the top and clicking on that section and removing that column. I leave the item name, the SKU, the UPC number and the price.

With this Excel spreadsheet, I create an extra column right next to the item. This way I can have a box to check if the item is there or not there. Then as I go through the box, I check the items that are in the box by placing an X in the column next to the item. Then if it's missing, I leave it blank. They do such a great job; I rarely find things missing except one time. I was missing 40 items, Liquidation.com forgot or missed shipping these boxes. They did refund me but it was dog food, and I wanted it for my pets.

When you first get your order from Liquidation.com open only one box as I said. Don't rifle through the boxes looking for something special. Take your time open up each box look at each item and put things out separately if you're doing as I did. First, I was doing this in my garage. I set up a table, and I put the box on top of the table. There was an empty box on the floor, where the damaged items went.

The good items in brand-new boxes went in one pile, and good items with damaged boxes went into another pile. Each time I found something I marked put an X on my excel spreadsheet next to it. If it was damaged, I put it D next to it, so I knew the conditions of each item. If I if it was broken, I marked it with a B. This way I know where everything is damaged pile, new pile, and broken pile.

Once I am finished with this box I move on to the next. Now I know the conditions of everything in this box. This keeps things simple. When I finished with this box, I went on to another. If my table became too cluttered I took all the new items and placed them in a box marked new. And the damaged box items were put in a box labeled as Used

Like New. Again this is my way, It's easy and straightforward, but you can do this in whatever way you like.

Now let's get to grading our items accurately. If it's a new box and it sealed don't open it. If it's a new box, but it may have been opened, you need to pull the item out very carefully to make sure that it works. If it works, put it back in the packaging precisely as you took it out and then go to the next item. Once you've completed, the new items list them all one by one by using UPC.

When you buy things from Liquidation.com, it's nice to have a heat gun or hairdryer nearby. A lot of times they'll come with labels over the UPC because they don't want you to be able to scan the UPC. These are closeouts, and they want them to be unusable.

With the heat gun or hairdryer, you can quickly remove those labels. I recommend you have a little trashcan by handy and remove those labels and trash them right away. You can use the barcode that's on the item. I suggest you punch the barcode into Amazon directly. The chance is 99 out of 100 that the barcode will work. On some rare occasion that it doesn't, then you have to look it up manually.

Go through your items one by one, since the new items you don't have to list the condition. Do your research. Put your price lower than other sellers. That is unless you don't want to sell the item. If that is the case, then you can price it whatever you want. But I assume the idea here is to sell the item. So you should price it less than your competition. After you finish with this item continue to the next item. Repeat this process until all your new items are done. Make sure you do all your new items first. That way you don't have any confusion or any mistakes.

Now you want to go to your new, but damaged box items. You want to look at each one of the items to see if you can fix the box and make sure that it seems new again. Again pulling anything out electronic anything out and looking at it to make sure it's working as new. Make sure that it is not cracked, broken or otherwise damaged. Maybe it was returned for a real reason.

Most likely it was returned because someone didn't want to read the instructions. It is likely that nothing is wrong with the item. Look at every piece of inventory to make sure all items are good and fully functional. This will save you feedback problems, and it will also save you from

Amazon problems. Look at everything so you can to make sure that it's in good shape.

If you want to be extra careful, then you can go to Staples or buy online these clear little round plastic circles that are tape. They look like what the manufacturer put on from the factory. If you look at something, and you realize it's new wrap it back up like it's supposed to be. Put it back in its plastic packing, put the wire ties back around it and make it look exactly like new.

Maybe someone pulled it out and didn't use it. You need to make sure it's new if you're sure it's new then wrap it back up. Put it back in the packaging, and then you seal it with another one of those little plastic stickers. Pull the old one off trying to get as close as possible to the original sealing tape. You're not cheating anyone; you are making it look new again. Be sure it looks new and work as new. And make sure the box is not damaged. If the box is damaged, then you can sell in as new but with a damaged box. Make sure you write a very good description.

Our next task is going through all the items that are new but have damaged boxes. This will be new open box, a box that you can't fix, but the item is still new. Now you may be able to list this as a new item but open box. Sometimes this category is there for Amazon sellers and sometimes is not. If it's not then you must list as used like new and put in a detailed description describing it as new. Something like this, "This item appears to be new. However, the box is damaged." You want to try and make sure that people understand that the item is a new item inside that damaged box. Once you finish, now you'll move on to your next category.

Selling items that are used is a challenge. You need to go through these items carefully; they may be broken. Go through each one of these used items to see if you can fix them. Once you get started, you may find that there is a duplicate item that you can take a piece off of to make it usable. Or you can keep it for yourself. A lot of times I'll find something that's broken, but I don't mind that it's broken. It does not bother me, and of course, it's free.

I have a very nice golf pen holder that's on my desk that the golf ball was broken off. There was no way that I could sell it to someone. This sells for over 200 dollars. I bought the order from Liquidation.com because I wanted that pen set. But unfortunately, it was broken. I didn't feel right gluing on the piece that was broken and shipping it out to a customer. I knew I would get negative feedback and the customer would get to keep the item. So I decided not to do that and kept it for myself. I ended up gluing the piece back on myself. Lo, and behold I'm happy with it and it has been like this for over three years now. It works perfectly, and I enjoy the pen.

Maybe you'll find something you want to keep because it's broken or damaged. Keep it. Enjoy it. Perhaps you'll see that it's broken, but not unusable. In that case, you go on to write your description. This item is used, and it has a chip off the right corner. The item would be new except for the chip. Therefore I'm marking it as used in good condition because it has a chip. If not for the chip it would be new. I will include the chip, and you may glue it on as needed if you so desire.

If you have a bedspread that has a small tear down the bottom, describe it well. Chances are no one will see it. But if you need it yourself, the take it, use it. Maybe your wife will fix it. You never know it. But if you sell it, some anal customer will find it and then try pressure you into giving it to them for free. Sell damaged items at your own risk. Now these damaged items can be sold on eBay with NO ISSUES!! See my eBay book for further details.

I have a fantastic pair of ski pants. These were Solomon pants, and they had a rip in the side. These were well over

$300 ski pants, but they had a tear in the side. Apparently, some idiot when they opened up the box cut them with a razor blade. Is it the perfect cut. I put a USA flag on it and off I went. I'm happy with a USA flag on the bottom of my pants, and no one will ever know. They may think I did it intentionally. There's no way I could sell those to a customer with a slit in them. They would they would not want to be seen in them. I personally don't mind.

So evaluate each item in your used or damaged box. If you can use it and you think you can sell it in good conscience to someone, then describe it accurately. If you have a beautiful little water bottle, but it has a dent in it at the bottom then explain it very well. And make sure it's very obvious that they are getting it a reduced price because it has a dent in the bottom.

I have lots of water bottles and coffee cups that are damaged. I'm afraid I couldn't sell them anyone without a complaint. I don't care, and other people out there may have the same feeling, they won't care. That being the case list it with full disclosure. If you think it's going to be a problem, then stop and don't sell it. It's not worth it, no matter what you sell it for.

I've sold things that I said were dirty and but still work. I had water feeder for animals it was for outside, and it was dirty. I marked this water feeder is as dirty, but still, works can still be used. Tested works as new but will need cleaning. The only thing you can see is when you open the box is how dirty this thing is. I was very worried about negative feedback on this one.

But sure enough, some guy bought it. I emailed him I said you realize this thing is dirty. I said I don't want you to be unhappy. He said I don't care I'm using it for the pigs. He got the item left me feedback that was positive. He noted the item was as described. Dirty and filthy but works, I am a happy customer.

I was happy I wasn't expecting that. I assumed he would say this thing too dirty. But really, who cares. It was a heated water feeder for the pigs. You throw it out there, and it keeps the water warm so the pigs could you drink from it. I was pleased that I found an intelligent customer, you don't see those all the time. A lot of people will still complain and say they were upset with the fact that it was dirty. They didn't to expect it to be that dirty but it's all in the perception of things.

Once you are finished with all your inventory go back to your spreadsheet and delete all the items not marked with a D. You will use that for the IRS, make a file someplace that says damaged items IRS tax write off. Verify the order number and place that at the top of your spreadsheet. Save this list on your computer and print it.

Use your Excel spreadsheet and assign a value to those items. You can leave the amount that came from Liquidation.com if you like. Discuss this with your accountant. I am not an accountant. Do what they say for the value. This will be a tax write off, but you need to verify this with your accountant first

But either way, keep that for your records and save it until the end of the tax year. Now bring the boxes and take them to any organization that you feel necessary and get a receipt. On that receipt, you want to mark the date that you received that order and the order number. Staple this to the back of your list or the front. Keep this in your tax file as well.

Now you have a record that you donated it, and you have a record of the items donated and their cost. So now you are good to go. You are ready to move on to your next task packing and shipping all the items you sold

Chapter 18 Adding Categories To Your Sales

Some categories on Amazon, beauty products, watches, coins and health items require approval. Those are in restricted categories, and you need to have permission to list in those categories. Health, beauty, and watches are relatively straightforward. Health aids like things to go around your legs, your arms and neck pillow things like that are a little harder. Some types of clothing are restricted items, and you have to have approval. You can find these by searching on Amazon seller central for restricted categories. Find the category that you're interested in and click on it. The procedures listed will tell you what you need to do to get approved in that category.

Most categories require that you show an invoice for purchases. Take note here; they will not accept your Liquidation.com invoice as a real invoice. Why, because it shows you purchased 84 miscellaneous items. The items are not listed in the way they will accept. However, the Amazon website says they will approve liquidation invoices. They will but only if you will show precisely the items purchased on your invoice. You will need to pressure your supplier to give you a proper invoice.

One particular category I wanted to get listed in was games. I bought a lot of about 400 games, and I tried to list them. They told me it was a restricted category. I went to the restricted categories, and I chose games and CDs. They again reminded me I needed an invoice. So I went back to the seller and had them create an invoice that showed my purchase from Liquidation.com.

You can create a fake invoice can if you wanted to but I wanted it as real as it could get. I'm not trying to deceive anyone. But I didn't have an invoice from anyone to show that all these things were purchased. At least in a specific format that Amazon will accept. So I had to ask Liquidation.com to modify the invoice. They created a new invoice complete with a phone number and listed the items individually that I purchased and the price paid.

Now I go back to Amazon, and I say I would like to sell these things. They said, please upload two invoices. Amazingly enough, I happen to have them, so I submit that my two invoices to them. A day later they sent me a message back saying one of the invoices was not accepted, but the other one was. I need to submit another invoice, but they would not tell me what was wrong with it. I have no idea. I asked, and they say I'm sorry we can't tell you what's wrong with the invoice, but it's not accepted. I found that strange since both the invoices looked the same.

So I asked Liquidation.com to make a new invoice, and I uploaded it again, A few hours later they responded that I was approved in this category, and it should show up in my list of available categories within the next 24 hours. It showed up right away, and I was able to sell things that day. I then listed all my games but I first made sure that they worked. I had my official game tester (my 12-year-old son) verify that the games worked. Once tested, I listed them all on Amazon.

Later I wanted to sell health and beauty supplies. The lot includes curling irons, hairdryers, things like that makeup mirrors. I bought an entire lot of 500 items from a different place, not Liquidation.com. It was a place called B stock. Now I have this lot of over 500 items of health and beauty supplies all brand-new in the boxes to sell. So I have to get approved in yet another category. I look at the requirements, and I find the items must be brand new. They must all be brand-new in the boxes for this category. If not then it must be marked as used and then go to eBay or some other website. You can't sell used in this category on Amazon, at least for now.

It sounds like a daunting task to do this, and yes it can be for the health and beauty supply category. But with perseverance, you can manage it. I reached out to B-Stock and asked them to create an Amazon-approved invoice. They did this for me very promptly, and I submitted these to Amazon. I sent over ten invoices from B-Stock in all. But Amazon keeps telling me that they're not they're not correct. There's something wrong with them, but they can't tell me what's wrong. So I keep resubmitting them and resubmitting them. Finally, I got someone to accept one of the previous ones that they told me wasn't right. After I resubmitted that one I started submitting the other invoices again. One by one, until I found someone who would accept another one of the invoices that they told me was not acceptable. All in all, I made 12 invoices, and they wouldn't take any of them. I didn't see anything wrong with them. But Amazon must have even though these were valid invoices directly from the seller.

Sometimes the people in Amazon don't see things, or they don't talk to each other. One person will approve something and the other will not. It is like you and me; we have different views and different opinions. They look for something small I guess that might show them that the invoice is a fake or a scam, I'm not trying to scam them. I just can't provide them with the invoice that they will accept. So I have to pressure the supplier to make an invoice to show that I do have legitimate title to these items. I purchased them fair and square, and all are brand-new in the box.

That is why they scrutinize every invoice to protect their name and customers. There may have been a number or a comma left out. Or the name of the manufacturer was spelled wrong. It was something like that; I never knew what was wrong. B-Stock listed everything including the company name, address, and all other information. They Included also that I paid by Visa card......***. And then put the last four numbers of my card and try to make it all look as normal as possible. But it took 12 tries to get it right. Don't give up, especially if you are right. Keep trying, and it will work out.

One time I wanted to add a new category, Food! I had bought a lot of food and wasn't like food per se food, but it was classified in the food category. I wanted to sell some of the things I purchased from a food wholesaler. What I wanted to sell was a Russian soft drink called, KVAS. It is like root beer except that it is not carbonated and it's an awful tasting to me. I don't like it, but a lot of Russian people I know love it, and so does my wife. She's European, and she likes it. It's something that Europeans have a taste for, but I don't care for it. There are many things that we will drink and eat that they won't drink, nothing wrong with KVAS but I don't care for it myself.

I had 54 of these bottles all brand-new never opened. I kept a few for personal use of course. But now how do I sell the rest. So I went to a local grocery store that sold KVAS. I bought ten different bottles of them; I asked the store manager to make me an invoice along with the tax. He obliged and printed me the perfect invoice along with his number. I went back home submitted the invoice to Amazon. Only a few hours passed and they replied. This time they told what was wrong was. I needed to have my name and phone number listed on the invoice. I knew I had to make the trip back down to the city and ask the manager to fix this. He again obliged, and I thanked him again for the service.

I then submitted that receipt to Amazon, and they accepted it right away. This was the most ridiculous thing you can imagine. But that receipt proves that I did go to the store and buy those so, therefore, I should be able to sell them. And ironically, people across the country who like the stuff want to buy it, and they pay good money for them. These bottles I purchased in the store are the same ones I bought in the lot. They sell for $5-8 each. It costs me $6 to ship each one, and I charge $8 for shipping. So I make 10-12 bucks on each one of these bottles.

So here it is, as you can see it pretty straightforward to get approved. Like anything, it takes time and following the rules to get it done RIGHT. If you have a specific question about opening up a new category, please email me. I will try to help and explain precisely how to do it. It is sometimes a difficult task, but working with Amazon is not hard if you try and be thorough. You need to understand this is their playground. And if you want to play, you need to cooperate and play by the rules. If you do, Amazon will help you as much as they can.

I want to mention here, that some categories require you to be on Amazon for a period of time, and you must have feedback above 98%. You must have no outstanding claims, and your ODR rate cannot be higher than 1%. If you come to one of these categories and click on it, they may say sorry, but your late shipment rate is below 96%. You cannot be approved for this category at this time. Please try to decrease your late shipping rate and then try again. This is a warning to you. Heed the warning and take care of business now and up front.

Okay, that sounds reasonable and easy, but don't say, Ok I'll do that tomorrow or maybe next week. I'll make sure everything gets out on time in the future. Don't do this make a change and do it NOW. Amazon does put performance restrictions in some categories to protect their buyers and sellers. Only you can fix a performance issue. If you don't, then you will eventually get booted off Amazon anyway, and you will never sell on Amazon again.

However, if your metrics are good then as you put in your inventory, you may get a message that says you need to be approved to sell in this category. Usually, this applies only to new items; typically you can sell used without any issues. If your metrics are excellent and you have been on Amazon long enough, you will be approved right away.

All that is needed is that you just click the button that says request approval. If all is ok the next screen will say that because you are in good standing, you have been approved. To list items in the newly approved category, all that you need to do is enter the UPC or item name again in the search engine box. Click search and this time you will see, that now you are eligible to list your items.

You have just crossed the step to the next level of Amazon. You are above the average seller; you now have more categories. That was easy right?

Additionally, some categories inside of categories require approval. One such category was Blue jeans. I wanted to sell the blue jeans that I purchased from Liquidation.com. I was approved in that specific category but not in the sub-category. Wow, that blew my mind. They told me I would have to ask for approval. I did show them an invoice from Liquidation.com. This time they accepted my invoice without me having to bug Liquidation.com into making a new one. The invoice this time did show 48 pairs of Calvin Klein jeans. Amazon accepted that invoice without question. Only God knows why. One day they take something, another day they don't, but hey it's done now, and that's all that matters.

Try new things on Amazon and try new categories. If you need to you can start out with the same standard categories as everyone. But eventually, you will find you have things that are restricted items. This doesn't mean that because it is restricted that you can't get approval. It says that you're not approved yet to sell there. Go check it out and see what the category requires. If Amazon needs you to complete some particular tasks, then finish them. It is all in your best interest anyway.

If you have a problem getting something approved, then email me let me look at your invoices. I'll be happy to try and help you. I will do my best to give you a couple of samples that I have that have gotten approved. With these, you can go from there.

Chapter 19 Other Wholesale Sources

Now there are real wholesale sources available. That is all new items so that you never have any problems with them at all. If this sounds great, you can try AliBaba.com this is a company owned by Google. There are several others, and I will list them at the back of the book that you can go through. But with Alibaba, you can buy brand-new items. Maybe you want to create your own brand. My wife especially liked their cosmetic lines, so I had ordered a few samples from this company. My wife loves cosmetics as do most ladies. She thought it was great, after considering the products for a few weeks we decided to make a move. I asked my wife if she wanted to create her own brand of cosmetics. She was so excited about the idea; I didn't realize how much it meant to her.

I immediately called the manufacturer and asked them how much would it cost for them to label the products with my brand name on them. And I needed an FDA certification and asked how long it would take to get this. Surprisingly they had the FDA certifications for the items I wanted. They said would put it on the side of the packaging for me. They could make labels with our own brand for only $0.10 per item if I ordered less than a thousand. But if I ordered 10,000 or more they would do it for free 10,000 was a hell of an amount to order. I spoke with my wife, and we went with only 5000. So that cost me $500 to have them labeled with her brand name.

Then I went to Amazon and went to their brand registry. I registered my items and listed my wife as the owner of the brand. I used the UPC's that I had bought as described earlier for the new items. Now she is the owner of that brand and the UPC. Now I can be the nasty person who calls and says hey this is my item and stop selling it. Although I could tell them that I own that UPC and you can't sell my items I probably won't. Because if they're buying them from me, I'm probably making money selling them to them, so I don't care.

After you've created your brand registry and before you can list your items you must show Amazon your FDA certification. We submitted these papers to Amazon, and within 24 hours we were ready to go. Now my wife has her own cosmetic eye cream along with her own eyeliner and mascara on Amazon all with her name on it. She can tell all her friends that she has her own cosmetic line now. Accomplishing this was so easy that she also decided to try makeup brushes. She found the perfect brush. It was over $90.00. We again called the manufacturer and asked if they could make brushes for us also, they replied yes.

They asked me to send them the brush she had purchased. I sent it overnight by FedEx, and after three days I had a call from my rep at the manufacturer. They had a sample ready and wanted to video chat with us. My wife loved the brush but wanted actually to see them and touch them

They offered to send it to their branch in NYC overnight. We said we would be there in the morning to see it. When we arrived in the morning, they had a whole line of brushes and already marked with her logos. She went crazy, and we signed a contract that day for 50,000 lots. They were set to arrive in 3 weeks. Now my wife has her own complete line of cosmetics and accessories. WOW!

After about six months she had someone come in from the cosmetic industry in New York and talk to her about her cosmetics. She also made a deal with the store in New York City to sell her cosmetics in the downtown store. She has many positive reviews on Amazon, but this type of attention was all entirely out of the blue. So there are places that you can buy things directly to make your own brand.

Then you be can be the sole owner of that brand and control the entire market.

That does not mean that you will own the entire market on cosmetics of course. But if you get enough people who are saying that your cosmetics are great, you will do well. Now I am merely using cosmetics; it could be a bowling ball, it could be ball bearings. It could be fishing rods or whatever you decide you want to sell. But please do your item research to see what works best for you, as I always say do your research, please. Find out how much it's going to cost how much and how much the shipping is going to cost. You will also need to check if there's going to be any import duties for your order.

There are loads of things to consider when venturing out into this area. Such as, how much are the items, and how much to get it branded in your name? How profitable will it be if you use their brand name for a while? Is that okay? And can they send you a letter from them saying you can use it? This way when you get cautioned by Amazon that you're selling someone else's brand, you can reply back to them that you are approved to sell this item. Then send them the letter, after that Amazon leaves you alone. They may harass you even if you have the letter in your hands. Because the manufacturer of those items doesn't recognize your name your screen, so you need to prove it. Once you have the letter, you are good too, and they will leave you alone then.

Amazon is all about the same thing that you do in everyday life. And that is you need to cover your butt to make sure everything is all lined up and ready. That way so that when someone says, excuse me, I have a question, you already have the answer. And you can hand it to them while saying thank you very much. Then you can move on to your general daily life.

The last thing you want to do is wake up and see that email from Amazon. We are sorry to inform you, but your account has been suspended. We have a complaint that you are violating the terms of service by selling products without the manufacturer's approval. Blah blah blah blah. That's all you need to have happened. Especially when Amazon is your only source of income. If so you will be broke until your Amazon account is up and running again.

Trust me it is a horrible feeling to have your Amazon account closed. You feel like the bad boy at the principal's office. Trust me I have been there. I know the routine. I know how it feels and it is not pleasant. Work within Amazon's guidelines, they are there to protect you from customer complaints and protect Amazon. This is all very understandable and easy to work with as long as you keep your cool.

Keep your ducks in a row and don't keep all your eggs in one basket. These are the same things I've told you before, and they apply to this as well. If you want to find something to sell on Amazon that is your own your own brand then do it. It can be stickers for skateboards, BMW logos for the hood of the car, whatever it happens to be. Just make sure you have a letter showing of approval to sell these items. And of course, you will need to buy your own UPC's. You can even have someone create your barcode's that will scan to match that UPC and start selling your items. It's a daunting task at first. It seems like it's just paperwork after paperwork, and you may not get it done. But you will, and then the hard work is done, now the easy job comes. Follow through and don't give up, keep going.

Amazon is a great place to sell, and most of the buyers are great. The Amazon reps will bend over backward to help you once they see that your good to your customers. I've had Amazon reps tell me secrets that they probably shouldn't tell me. Things about how information is tracked. Be good with Amazon and Amazon will be good to you. This is a simple rule to follow.

Now another excellent source of products is the trade show circuit. I attend a lot of wholesale trade shows. When I do go to trade shows, I tend to look for smaller manufacturers. In many cases, the owner of the company is right there in the booth. At the last Seattle Gift show, we found a small jewelry company that makes everything in the USA. Both owners were at the show. I asked if they sold to eBay and Amazon sellers and they said they did not. After discussing the opportunity, we made a deal to buy only their jewelry. They also agreed to sell only to us for Amazon and eBay. Great for both of us in all senses of reality.

Trade shows offer the opportunity for you the small buyer to make deals upfront and in person with the actual seller. These are excellent sources for new products for you. I will place a list of trade shows in the back of the book and online for you.

Chapter 20 Buy Closeouts At Retail Stores

Finding great deals for your Amazon account can be as near as your local retailer. I came out of the local pharmacy store, and I'm headed over to another pharmacy store. I'm buying a load of Christmas lights and Christmas decorations. I went in to get some headache pills, but I saw all the Christmas lights the kind for outside your house, the laser type. They were 75% off those things are $29 apiece I'm now buying them for less than $10. In fact, I spent $250 on for inventory at the CVS.

Now that merchandise is not that is not going to make me any money until next Christmas. Maybe I will list them early starting next November. So I will hold on to the merchandise until then. I'm now heading over to another store, and then I will head over to one of the famous hardware stores and see what they have. Yes, this is something I often do.

When you buy things like this, it is called arbitrage. You are making money by purchasing thinks the store can't or didn't sell. It costs too much for them to send it back, so they get rid of the items at a discount. I will do this because I'm getting brand-new unopened items. And I a am buying them at way less than it would cost me if I would buy these from a regular wholesaler. If I purchased these wholesale, they would cost me $20, and I could sell them for $30. Right now I'm getting them for about seven dollars. But when Christmas rolls around next year, I'll sell them for $30. I'll make $23-$25 on each one of them.

I often browse the local hardware stores and other retailers to see what they have in their clearance aisle. Last month I bought 30 door lock sets for $12 each. I listed them from my car before I left the parking lot and had four sold at $49 by the time I was in my warehouse. By the end of the day, I had sold 10 and recouped my investment and made a profit.

You can go to any of the major retailers and do this. But I find that hardware stores are my best source. I often buy tools at 10-20% of retail. These are new items in the box, so no complaints here from nasty customers. Try it yourself and take off any day, cruise around to any store and look for clearance items. You will find a gold mine.

Here is an example, perhaps you see something in a store, sitting on a shelf that's clearance. If you look closely and know your market, then you will look at it you'll know exactly how much you can sell it for on Amazon. And if you see 10 of them, you will almost scream with joy. I found Garfield phones one time walking into a discount store. Garfield is still very popular here in America. I bought them at retail for about a dollar apiece. I sold them all for 25 bucks the same day. I only had 15 of them, and after they sold, I went from store to store to store to find more of them. I didn't it felt awful that there weren't more, it was very horrible.

Chapter 21 Take It Slow

Getting loans to fund your Amazon

I had money to start my Amazon business. In fact, if I lost it, I probably would've been irate. I wasn't rich by any chance, but I had some money to start my Amazon account, and I sold some things around my house to build some Amazon feedback and create some additional cash. These were things that I didn't need, that's the best way to generate some extra cash.

While I am on the money issue, I will tell you that there are many companies out there that will offer you money. PayPal funds one of them, a couple of them are supported by other organizations. They will provide you with cash to use, Amazon has offered me money, as much as $20,000 to buy inventory, but the interest rate is so unbelievably high that it is not even funny. They show the interest rate at a low rate, but somehow they compounded it, they twist it, they shape it into a higher rate.

I don't know how they do it but if you take $4000 and you end up paying 5200 back. Now if I take $4000 of items typically, I will make $8 to 10,000 on that money. So my 4000 becomes $8 to 10,000 in sales. If I just make my minimum of $8000 and then I need to turn around and give somebody $1200 of my profit. Now while it's still good, and you can make money with other people's money, it is still a bite off of your face.

I do know someone who took money from one of these places. I won't name the company for apparent reasons. He received $4000 from this company to buy stock for his new store. After he had paid about half of it down, they offered him another $5000. He felt since he was doing so well on Amazon that it was an excellent opportunity. Then suddenly his $4000 became $10,000, and he finally was stuck paying back 16,000. I start pointing out to him that you know you're paying back too much in your profits, You are going to make on the $10,000 last lot of items that you bought. But you still owe them $16,000. You are creating a best that beast that can never be satisfied.

And more importantly, someone else is making money off your hard work. He thought he could beat the system and pay it off early. Human nature is that it's only a $600 payment or It's only $1000 payment, I'll just pay the thousand dollars, and I'll catch up the next time and then the next time rolls around. I'll catch up the next time, and the result is you don't catch up. The result is you end up paying $16,000 for the $10,000 that you borrowed, and you've lost all your profit, and that's what he did. He couldn't pay the loan back. He ended up selling all of his Amazon stuff and still owed them $3000. He had nothing left except to take money off of his credit card to pay them.

Then he called me up and told me my system didn't work. I showed him my new car told him my house had no mortgage. I told him I had a home in Florida and that I'm sitting on my deck right now while the kids are outside playing in the pool. I said my system works; you just took risks that I won't make.

Eventually, he got over his anger with me and told me that I was probably right, and he knew the system worked. He said he would like me to set down with him and start again and go through everything with him again. That was three years ago. Now he is one of Amazon's top-rated sellers. His wife makes little things in NC and sells them on Amazon. He's now a top rated seller on eBay with over 10,000 items listed by merely following the right procedures. These procedures are proper for most people; you may have to adjust them to your needs or to your circumstances to your way of thinking. However, this is what works for me, change this to match your needs. This is only here as an example to give you an idea where to go.

When we started again, he started out with $1000 from his credit card. I helped him buy the right things. I helped him inventory them and go through them to categorize them. I showed him the right way to classify them. Those conditions are, New in the box, New open box, Used like new, Used very good, Used good and Used acceptable. Some items may be collectible and have different conditions.

I showed him how to do all that in two weekends, and once we did that he was able to get back on track. His first $1000 made him $2500 profit. That's his thousand dollars back to his credit card and $2500 in profit. Then he turned around and took that $2500 and placed more orders. His next $1000 order made him $4000 in profit this time. That's a hell of an increase for $1000. But I told him to slow down and take your time, don't get ahead of yourself again. Take your time and get the experience doing it right!! Start slow.

By this time he had a pretty good system going. When he brought in the next inventory order, he was ready. He was using tomato boxes at the start and then eventually went on to buy some real plastic boxes. I told him the tomato boxes were fine and he purchased these only so he would feel better about how his inventory was kept. He agreed, but this was ok.

Then he sold that lot and made $4200 in profit. Again he was ready to go and jump whole horse into it and buy a $4000 order of merchandise. I said no take your wife out to dinner, and go someplace relax for the weekend. Go to the city and stay in a hotel and have a beautiful night out. Come back see me on Monday, and we will buy some more inventory.

Monday came, and he was very relaxed and told me he was ready to go. As we sat down, I could see he was starting to see the bigger picture. He knew now that he had to check out what will sell and what will be sold quickly. And what is the profit you will make with the items? It all must make sense BEFORE you buy. Now he sees where he will end up.

When he ordered this time, I let him buy $4000 worth of inventory. He saves on shipping since the warehouse is close to us. He asked me if I would drive out with him in his truck so we can go pick up the order. It's only 400 miles away, so I said sure we would make a day trip out of it. We left early the morning, and we arrived by noon. They loaded everything for us on his trailer while we went out to lunch. We were home by 8 PM. It was a long day, but I helped a friend, and I helped someone who has helped me many times.

Now he's doing great; he is a super seller on Amazon, a power seller on eBay. And yes my friend does compete against me sometimes, but there's plenty of customers out there who will buy from me because I have over 10,000 feedback when he has only around 2000. And there are others who will buy from him because he's cheaper than I am. It's all okay. There's plenty of business on Amazon for everyone.

I would mention his name, but I promised him I wouldn't. If you knew it, you would know who he is because he does so well. I also won't mention my screen names on Amazon or eBay because I don't want some vindictive person to go out and buy something from me just to ruin my account and believe me somebody will. Some other seller will think I'm telling their secrets about Amazon so I won't do it. Someone would do it for vengeance.

The moral here is start slow work your way into it. Once you see you're getting it, you can move at a faster pace. When you see you understand it, you can buy more inventory. Do not go out and run up your credit card to buy $1500 worth of stock and say what do I do now? You will end up with $1500 of items and have it all stuck in the garage and not know what to do with it. Trust me it will not work that way because you will get bored. Place one order at a time, that's two boxes maybe three boxes sometimes.

Go through it until you figure out what you're doing. Once you know what you're doing what you got it under control, you can double your order. The next time you can increase your order and keep doubling your order until you get up to the point where you do have $10,000 in the bank you can afford to blow hundred blow $4000 and by a huge lot.

Remember to go through your order box by box, use the same procedure one box at a time. Don't open up ten boxes or you won't know where you are in the process. Create your file from Liquidation.com and open up the box with the right number on it. The numbers are categorized by the auction which you purchased these that's how Liquidation.com does pull that out go through that list. Find the items that are there mark them appropriately and then get those items listed. Go through each box and follow the same procedure.

Maybe once you get situated, and you understand how this all works you can change this. Perhaps you can open up all the boxes at one time and spread them out. I will tell you that even I don't quite do that, but I will open up four or five boxes at once. Right now I have several employees we all open up the boxes and spread them out or n a large work area. We have a table for damaged items, and we have a table for new items. We have one big work area in the middle where we will open up all the boxes. We go through and pull the inventory out one by one, piece by piece, and categorizes them. Then someone else goes back through and checks the categorization to make sure they were all accurate.

We just want to make sure that someone did not shove something in the new box knew that they thought was new but it's damaged. And that something didn't get into the used box that's damaged or new. These things can happen. I also have someone going along and heating off the labels to reveal the UPC label. One guy is an expert at it, with a little bit heat he can pull them off with no effort.

Next someone else comes along grabs the item and takes it over and lists it on Amazon. He works with one box at a time. He just keeps going until the boxes are full or he runs out of products to list. Someone else,(usually me) separates them for the different categories in which I list.

Typically each order that I get are pretty much all the same items, so it's not necessary to break them apart and pull them apart. If I order fish and pet supplies, they are all in the same box. If I order clothing, it's all in the same box. Rarely do I find the merchandise mixed up. Although sometimes they are and I have to break them apart, separate them and put them in different places.

If your order is huge then you may have too much of a mess, you may not have enough space on your tables. That is unless you have large tables. You may end up mixing things up and end up with negative feedback. So be careful and double check your inventory and conditions.

Try to keep it small and under control. If it was just you and your wife who are doing this together, then it is easy to manage. Try to keep everything in an organized fashion until you get the hang of it. Once you get the hang of everything's, you can go full blast. You can modify this any way you want, but the critical thing here is to start off slow. Get your feet wet understand to see how things work and then adapt this method to fit your needs better. You're the one that's in control. You're the one that needs to figure out how you want to get it. Not too hard. Take it slow, move on slowly get the hang of it, then you can go as fast as you want.

To go over the points again!

Take it slow.

Don't take money to buy inventory that you can't pay back.

Don't open more than one or two boxes at a time.

Take it slow.

Take it slow.

Chapter 22 Starting Your Own Brand.

If you're interested in being unique and starting your own brand, you can, and Amazon is the place to do this. There are numerous companies which I have listed at the end of the book will help you achieve your goal. The specific one that I can tell you about right now would be AliBaba.com. You can create an account and then go to their website and put in a request for quote or an RFQ. You need to know that term; it's an RFQ. Say for example you want to sell a water sprinklers and you want your sprinkler to be a specific type. So you go on to AliBaba.com you search for water sprinklers. When you search, you will find some very similar to the brands that you can find at any of one of the major stores in America.

Then try one out, see what you like about it. Once you are an expert, then you can go to Ali Baba.com and ask for a quote on one similar to what you want. Chances are you'll find one exactly as you want and if not, you can ask them to make a design change. Now a design change would, of course, cost money but it's not as expensive as you might think. They would have to retool and make a few changes. But if you're serious about this, that may be something that interests you.

But if all you want is to have it branded is your name, then find one that you like the features that you like. Find something like one of the top brands like Orbit and Raintree. Perhaps you want to name yours something completely different. Or maybe you want to have it with your name or brand. This way with your specific personal name everyone knows it's yours. Now you can do that; you can ask the people who are selling these things to brand them up with your logo or your label. You are now the boss.

And if you don't have a logo, go to fiver.com ask someone there to make you a logo they'll do it for 15 or $20. You need to give them an idea what you have in mind. Once they finish, you will have your specific logo, and you have that logo placed on your new sprinkler. Now everyone knows it's yours. Have your phone number and all your information stamped onto the back with another. These folks will do that for you, and yes they will charge you. Not too much of a price but they will charge you. However it's worth it.

My wife had something specifically made for her. She had her brand name and label added to the product. They charged her $0.10 per item since she was ordering only a thousand. At that time it was only $500 to have a label put on the product with her name and her logo on it. That's pretty impressive when she eventually got up to ordering 10,000 they did for free. They figured if she's going to order that many they'll do it for her at no cost. She kept asking them to reduce it, and finally, they said will do it at no charge for her. Eventually, they put two logos on; and they embossed her logo on the items. Then they put her phone number company information on another label.

Now my wife had a brand-name item with her brand name. You can do the same. We are using sprinklers here as an example, but you could use anything. It could be cables for iPhone's or whatever you want as your item. Look on Amazon you will find 50 people with different names all selling the same cable. Some of them are generic cables with no information on them. Some of them have their brand name embossed on the cable. This may cost a little bit for a starting seller, but it will pay you back. When your buyer rips the end off; he will remember your name and buy it from you again. Brand name recognition is essential. It's good marketing; No it's outstanding marketing. You need to decide if you're ready for that upfront or if you want to wait for later.

Then when your regular stock has been depleted, you can start selling your new stock with your logo on them. This is not rocket science, and this is not hard to do. My wife recently purchased 50,000 items from her supplier. When she asked for a different logo on the new items, they did so at no cost, because she ordered such a large quantity. It was the cheapest that she ever purchased her stock. It was even half of what her original purchase was. How can they sell these products so cheap? And most are good quality products at this price, this is unbelievable.

My wife purchased scarves this time with her name or logo embossed onto the scarf and a tag on the scarf sewn in with her name. So they must've made 50,000 labels and gave them to the people who were sewing and had them put on for her. This is simply an amazing process.

We went to China to the factory and met the people making them. They were very friendly people, and they put us up in their corporate hotel at no cost. We paid for expenses to get there of course, but they realized we were doing a 50,000 item deal, so they wanted to impress us. Now 50,000 items was a lot for us. But she purchased them for a $1.25 apiece so, in the great corporate sense, it doesn't seem to be like a lot of money. It was nearly $65,000 plus the shipping cost of about $ 400. The even made special clear packages with her labels on them as well. They did this without asking, and it was cool. This was already prepared for a retail store, so if she ships them out to retail, then they are all ready to go.

I'm using my wife as my example, and the sprinkler is an example. However, you can use any item you want if you want to sell bookbinders then do so. You can buy bookbinders and have your name put on them instead of the popular brands that you see all the time. Now you can have Dave's bookbinders or Dave's best bookbinder. Whatever you want, you create a brand for yourself you, and you own that brand. If you see someone selling Dave's best and you know you did not authorize anyone to sell Dave's best, then you can tell them they can't sell your item. Now you can be the one sending the nasty letters out. You can be telling Amazon that this is your brand and no one can sell your item.

Now you don't have to do this maybe you don't care. Especially if someone bought the items from you, they decide they want to sell it. Let them do this; it's okay. Now if someone's faking and copying your item selling cheap knockoff's, then you have to take action. But it's all up to you, why? Because it's your brand, you control if you are the owner of that brand.

An added benefit is the bragging rights of your brand name items. Now, this may not be your entire agenda, but would it be nice when someone asks you what you do. Like with my wife for example. People ask what do you do? She replies I have my own brand of cosmetics on Amazon. I also have my own brand of accessories on Amazon. While bragging rights may not be necessarily your goal, it is impressive in the business world that you have a brand of your own. Not only do you sell on Amazon but you have your own brand, your own line of something.

People then tend to give you a little more respect, even if it's your own brand of cables or your own brand of guitar picks. You can say I sell my own brand of guitar picks exclusively on Amazon. Now you sound like a big person, maybe that's not your goal. But these things are all good for extra points.

Alibaba is but one of the sources where you can get new items or your own branded items. I will give you a list of wholesale suppliers. They will put you on their list. They will send you different wholesale magazines based on your needs. You want textiles; you can get textiles. If you want furniture, you can get furniture. If you want clothing, you can get clothing. My wife also has jackets explicitly made to her specifications. She has them in various sizes, various colors, and different thread designs. She even regulates it down to the type of thread she wants. They will make them for her specifically for her. They are her brand. Her brand name is sewn in the linings, and her name is sewn inside the pockets on a small tag. These are her jackets, anyone that picks up one of these jackets knows it is hers. The moment they pick it up they see it right away because it is embossed with her brand. Now she's not Versace, but everyone who is in this industry who sees these know who she is and knows her brand

So if this is a niche that you want to get into and you want to have your own brand, you're good to go. You can create yourself a website based on your brand, and you can build yourself a following based on your brand. Just like anything, the more you promote it, the more it works for you. If you think only putting on Amazon is good enough, then that's great. But in reality, it's not enough. Yes, you're right, people will find it, and yes people will eventually start to buy your product. But do you want to wait till everybody finds your item or do you want to shove it right in front of their face, so they all see it?

This is how marketers make their product accessible. They cram it down your throat, this way everyone sees it this way, everyone is ready to buy your brand when it's ready. My wife was marketing her cosmetics for six months before selling them. She had samples she was sending out people. She was at cosmetic shows and fairs; people were talking about her cosmetic line before it was even available for sale. She would send out samples, and she would get reviews on her brand online. She would ask them to post the positive comments and positive reviews then.

Then came the launch date for the cosmetics, her brand name was ready. Now again I'm not going to tell you the name because I am not plugging my wife here, This is no different than the fact I refuse to plug anyone else in this book. Her brand name cosmetics were available on sale on Amazon for pre-order the day before launch. She had hyped the brand so much that people were begging for the item early.

Because she had done so much hype, because she had done so much advertising and because she had prepped so much the opening day her pre-order was a success. She sold 20,000 units in the first five days that quite honestly paid for the entire order. As a matter of fact, she was short about 5,000 units after three more days. She was short 30,000 units in less than 30 days. She had sold over 100,000 units of her cosmetics. The first day she sold 8000 which was one-third of her stock on that day.

After five days she made an urgent phone call, she spoke to the factory manager, and she placed an immediate rush order. She wanted everything she ordered the first time doubled and she needed it right away. It cost her extra for the rush, but by Friday only three days after the phone call, she had an order on the way. This saved her new company. They were able to get those things in a box and get them out by FedEx. This cost her way more than the original price, and the shipping was three times as much. However, by Monday she had another 50,000 units in hand.

However, when they arrived, they were almost all sold by the pre-orders. So she made another call and ordered 100,000 units no rush, but she did pay for Fed Ex shipping. In 10 days she had another 100,000 units in hand. But again these things were selling so fast; She figured out it was not enough. She yet placed an order for 200,000 units, No rush, no special shipping this time. But in 3 weeks she had sold almost half of the order that was arriving. She once again called and placed a demand order of 50,000 units each week.

Believe it or not, that was just enough for the demand she had created. She also wanted specific items which she could see were selling to have those items increased. She wanted 10,000 of these items, 5000 of these, 10,000 these and she wanted that every week until further notice. That way it was on automatic. My wife now sells over 200,000 units of her own brand name cosmetics every month. Without all this extra work she would probably be selling the 10 or 20 units a week.

That's what everybody else does with their own brand name items. They just hope that people will find their item on Amazon and make millions. But in reality, the gods of selling do not work this way. You are rewarded when you market your items. And if you don't market, then you will not be paid. Amazon marketing is what you need to do, now as I said, I worked as an analyst for a company I was there in marketing. I know how to do that, so yes I did do all of the marketing that for her. That's one of the things I do best.

However, you can hire people and fiver.com or on freelancer.com to market your cosmetics. They will go to blogs or do podcasts about your cosmetics. Maybe even to do an infomercial, it's not that expensive. I think all in total with all the things that we did for promotion we spent less than $5,000. And I did also use some people from Fiver.com since they had more experience in specific areas than I did. I let all the other people do the work that I felt would end up better for her.

It was all worth it however since she since on opening day she had sold 20,000 units of cosmetics. That's impressive in anyone's eyes. I think anyone would be happy with the results since she went from nothing to selling over $5 million in cosmetics in less than a year. She expects next year based on the continued growth of her product that she will sell approximately $10 million in cosmetics. Think about it this all started from nothing. It all started with me asking her what would she like to sell on Amazon.

And of course, since she was on her way to her favorite store to buy cosmetics, she said how about selling cosmetics. I said sure, and we sat down in front of the computer and said ok find what you want to sell. I had already put her on the Alibaba site. I said you find what you're looking for and then we will make it happen and the rest is history.

I'm telling you this because my wife is not a business person. My wife never held a job. My wife only did charity work because I had an excellent corporate cushy job. So if my wife can think up something to sell with no business experience, and if my wife can take the $5000 she spent on the cosmetics and make money then you can too.

This was a gamble, and yes it was a lot of money at that time. If you take the $5000 for advertising and $ 5000 we spent on products to sell, we had $10,000 into a gamble. But that gamble paid off. She made money back the first day. Now she can divorce me and be well-taken care. I hope she doesn't read this and get any ideas.

We could have spent less, but I wanted to take a chance, And it paid off, very well. And my wife is a mother and wife with no business experience. Now she is doing infomercials and running with prominent people in the cosmetic industry. If she can do it so can you. It's there and it's available; you have to want to do it.

And as I said if you think you're going to sit around and wait and hope for the best you will be sadly mistaken. You'll be like every other Tom, Dick, and Harry out there who gets nothing done. I have trained people on the system, and I know what they do. They put everything out, they do everything in the way I tell them to do, then sit back and do nothing. They expect it all to be magical. It's not magical unless you consider advertising as magic. Everything is about advertising and advertising is all about marketing. If you sit around and wait, it won't happen. Yes perhaps maybe eventually somebody will find your products fascinating or needed. Perhaps somebody will be interested in it enough to make some comments, and off you go.

But more likely your item will just fade away into oblivion. Do you want that? If not then get off your ass and go for it!!

Chapter 23 Amazon Associates And Marketing

Amazon Associates is a quick way for you to make more money. There are so many discounts that are available for different groups. Let's say perhaps you want to go to a college blog and post that you can get them a discount on software at Amazon. You can put your link on their blog, and you may get a few sales from Amazon that way, and the students will also get a discount. When they buy, you will get a 3 to 5% maybe sometimes 8% of that sale now that's not much but if you make a 100 or you make 500 transactions you've done pretty good.

You can go to Amazon and sign up for an associates account, and they will give you a link to post in anyplace you like. I will post a list of Amazon links in the back of the book. The only requirement is that you tell them where you're going to post their links. They won't restrict you, but they do like to know where you're putting them. They obviously don't want children's clothes on porn sites. I'm sure you get the idea.

Go to Amazon set yourself up and ID you create yourself a website that you're going to market your links. But you can place your links anywhere. Anyplace you put your Amazon ID is a good idea. And anytime someone buys off of your link even if they don't buy the item you linked to you still get paid. So if you send someone there to look for books, they end up going and buying a stereo or they end up going and buying clothes you still get a percentage of that sale. I end up getting a percentage of the original transaction because they did purchase something.

Amazon and ClickBank are big now. I know people who are making 1500 to 2000 dollars per month. I have four accounts myself. Yes, I do make money off these links too. So yes, I know it works. So don't say I'm being a consultant and trying to tell you something that I've not done. I have done this, and I do make money off of these links myself. When I fell out of the corporate grace, I did everything I could to bring income into my family.

When I first started out I made about one hundred dollars from this website. But it was like gold to me. I originally had four or five sites bringing me $100 a month, and it didn't require me to make a lot of effort. I just had to go on and post a few blogs here and there. I posted a few comments to drive people back to Amazon. And yes, eventually I created more prominent posts and larger blogs. Now I have someone who posts all of these links for me. So yes I do know how to do this, and yes, I have done it for myself.

Amazon gives you all the tools you need to make money. Why does Amazon do this? Because Amazon wants to make money and if they help you, then you both will succeed. Think of Amazon as the dad you are the child. Amazon is giving you everything you need now you're the adult. All you have to do is take what they have and go with it; Amazon is giving it all to you right there in your hands. All you have to do is grab it and use it. Amazon will let you make links on just about any category.

Amazon will also give you money if you send people to their website and they sign up for prime membership. And when people sign up, they get a free month of prime membership. Also, Amazon will send you five bucks when they make their first purchase. Amazon will send you a piece of these customers purchases for as long as they purchased first using your link. This is a win-win situation.

Amazon wants you to succeed in Amazon will give you all the tools for you to succeed. You just have to take them there. There is an entire page of offers for you to choose from. For example, if you know people who are getting snap benefits or also known as food stamps in the old vernacular, they can get Amazon prime for $5.99. Normally this is $10.99 per month, and most people don't know this.

But if you market that to the right people or if perhaps you go to a local food bank, you can get loads of sign-ups. If you can get this information out there for those people, you might get some sign-ups. You get your link out for these people to for Amazon prime at only $5.99 a month. They may be paying $11 a month right now. Now saving five bucks over a year comes to about $60. Now maybe that's gas in the car twice. Or perhaps dinner one night, but seriously money is money, I have been there $60 can be a lot to some people. So here is a chance for you to make money for yourself and save people money.

You have to work again to accomplish things here. I know I said that horrible, horrible, degrading four letter word work. I know it was awful of me to mention that again, but it is work. But you know what you can do, and you can get your wife to do it also. When my wife was still working the charity work, I started getting her to do this for me to do this for me. She posted links here and posted these links there, and you know what she liked the work. It's not hard work if you like the computer and you like hanging around reading the comments on Yahoo.

It's the same thing as when you find a blog that's interesting about science fiction; you see a popular science fiction book on Amazon you go there in your post a link to the book with your ID. If somebody buys it, then you get a piece of it. It's not much, but a thousand pieces are better than nothing. And if you're on a blog and that has 80,000 people and only 1% of them like your post, and if that 1% do buy from your link, then that's a lot of cash.

But again all of these things require marketing, so you do have to do something. Even with this book right here, the one that I'm telling you about needed marketing. If I just threw it out on Amazon and expected someone to find it, I would still be waiting, and you would not be reading this. Yes, someone would find it, yes, and it would sell. And yes I would be a published author, and I could brag to my friends about how well I'm doing while I'm still working at the grocery store as a checkout clerk or whatever.

The bottom line is, everything requires some level of marketing, however much you put in is however much you get out of it. So if you think you're going just to float along and do a little bit of marketing here and there it won't work. That's how your business is going to is be, it will just going to float along and make a little money here and there. The more you market, the more you sell, the more you sell, the more you can afford to market. This means the more you can sell, this creates a loop, and you're the only one that can make that loop. This is where it's all up to you.

You are your own boss now!!

Chapter 24 How To Market Your Products

Marketing is all about you. You want it or if you don't want it. Marketing is still all about you. Now marketing is something you need to get into for profit's sake. In reality, it is not very complicated. The best thing you can do is if you don't know anything about marketing but you want to learn is hop on the Internet. There are plenty of books you can download. There are plenty of tutorials on how to market. It's funny when you get into this that there are so many things you can do to sell your items for yourself.

Marketing is not as complicated as it seems, especially the type of marketing you're going to be doing. You're just going to be promoting the products that you already have. It's not like in the environment where I was when I had a new product that was created and had to start from scratch. We had to design an ad campaign around that product and then sell it to people who've never heard of the product before, this was a daunting task. Sometimes you had to make people believe and have confidence in your product that had just magically appeared. So that's more difficult.

This type of marketing getting is pretty simple. You need to find a place to make an advertisement; then you need to find a place to push traffic towards your listings. More importantly, you need to find a way to get people to convert, which means in the marketing world to buy your product. If you have a thousand people that look at your listing, but only one buys your item, then that's a very poor conversion rate. Whereas, on the other hand, if you have 100 people look at your website and three buy, then that's a high conversion rate.

Now it depends on how and who you market to. If you go in and let's just say you market your high-end bicycle to people who buy romance novels your conversion rate will be probably zero. You might get lucky there might be someone there who reads romance novels and has a family that wants to buy a high-end bike for their family. There's always that possibility, and by the same token, you don't want to go in and market to the romance novels to the swimwear market. Your romance novels may sell a few, but it's not going to be a targeted audience.

So you must target your audience correctly that is your priority. You must find out what it is you're trying to sell via your links. If you're selling just general Amazon items, then that's very easy. You go on to various consumer boards post a few links; you go to a few blogs post a few links. Or go to a few websites post a few links directly going to your store. Now you start marketing to specific lines to market.

If you decide to go into a line of swimwear and that's what you want to sell you would go to swimming websites, swimming forums, swimming blogs. I think you see where I'm going. I don't think I have to dwell on this and shove it down your throat, you market to the people who might be interested in your product that doesn't mean other people won't buy your product by far. I've bought women's bras, and I'm a guy, but I bought something for my wife. I have bought women's perfume; I bought my lady shoes once. So you can see there are exceptions to that rule.

You may be you may be targeting a soccer mom who likes to drive a Corvette, so she wants cool things for her car. You may be targeting a senior citizen group who has animals and pets, and they want to buy pet products for their pets. Soccer moms are your bread-and-butter; they are the ones who are going to buy clothes for the children and household items. They are the ones who are going to buy the sheets, the bedspreads and the appliances around the house. They are the ones who are going to buy those things off of your Amazon link website.

That is not to say that a man will not go there and buy some things as a gift or even buy them for himself if he likes an item. We also can't say that if you market tools to the gentleman, that a woman will not buy something for herself that she or for someone she likes. I am not going to push on this too much, but I think you get the idea market to your target audience.

Do your research. All you have to do is log onto the internet and if its swimming items then you need to search for swimming blogs. You can probably find more than you can read in several days. These are where you will market your swimming products. I say swimming simply because I chose that product; it could be any product. So don't get confused by me referring to swimming as if you were only doing swimming products. Only market to those places that are properly in your market. You have to be polite about it. If you go in and spam the blogs or websites and put in 20-30 links a day, you're going to end up with a problem. Most of these boards will ban you if you post too many links in a day and rightfully so, your spamming these boards. In reality, these boards are there for people to share information and ideas not to advertise your products. You can, but you have to be gentle about it.

Your best bet is when you come onto one of these bulletin boards to just read and watch what's going on. See what the active topics are about and see what people are saying even if you have no interest in what's going on. Open up a dialogue with the people make a comment or two. Find something that you think you can make an intelligent comment about and say something about it. Wait for a reply. Maybe won't get one until a couple of days later, then make another comment. Then a few days later, comment and post your swimming links.

Just post about your favorite things and why you like them. If people go there and look at that favorite thing to see what you're interested in maybe, they won't like it, but maybe they will. And maybe just maybe they'll buy something, even if they go to that link and they buy a refrigerator you still get a piece of that. It doesn't have to be what you sent them to the site for, and the cookies from their visit will stay with them unless they clear the cookies. These cookies remain there for weeks or months, and you will get paid every time they go to Amazon buy something.

However, if you go on these boards and you post several links without making any comments as far as everyone's concerned you are a spammers and they will treat you as such. And they will block you. Maybe you won't notice it, you'll still be able to go on there, and you'll still be able to post, but unfortunately, your posts will not be seen by anyone. It's what they call ghosting; you look at your post when logging on. You look at your post, and you're happy. No one else sees it, however, only you can see it. If you would log off your computer and log in from another computer and look for that post, it wouldn't be there. It would be gone because they ghosted you. Craigslist started this many years ago when people started spamming. They let the spammers think that they were posting all their little links and everything. However, eventually whatever they posted was just ghosted and not seen by anyone at all.

Now there are lots of solutions to go out and post these things automatically, but you can do them manually. You can pay someone on fiver.com to do it for you, and they may have quite honestly better access to people than you do. I've seen some people who say they'll post your link to 80,000 people targeted and they know where to target them. That's good and for 10 to 15 bucks, that not a bad price. One or two sales and you made your ten dollars back and hopefully; you'll make more than that. With 80,000 that's a lot of people who will see your link, and I've seen people brag they have 400,000 subscribers to their podcasts and websites.

The advantage to using someone for fiver.com or one of the other services is that these people make sure you do not get ghosted. Most submit your link to their subscribers, and they don't get over market things. Some are selective and may reject what you're giving them to market for you because it's not in their line.

I do the same thing if it doesn't meet my subscriber's needs I will not send it out. I have over 50,000 subscribers now. I know if I send them junk they will not be interested and will eventually unsubscribe. My valued subscribers will go someplace else because I am sending them crap that they are not interested in at all. If you send them targeted emails with things that are along their lines of thinking, then they will not be offended and may buy from one off my list. So keep that in mind. One of these services might be a good idea to get started in until you get your own blog, and you build up your list of followers. This is just simple marketing; this is not your high-end marketing. This is just straightforward stuff.

As I said I don't plug a lot of people, but I will plug fiver.com because it is just full of average people like you and I using their talent to help others. Fiver.com is an excellent place to look for talent. If you happen to be a person who can translate documents, then you can place your ad on Fiver.com. Fiver.com charges the person who places the ad a little bit when someone hires your services, and then you get paid for it. I have found proofreaders here and had people here make book covers for me. I have most of my book covers done by people on fiver.com. I had one done by someone else, and I can tell you that that was a far, far superior product and the service was great. However, it was ten times the amount it cost me on fiver.com to get one done. So I could get ten books done on fiver.com. I think I could change the book cover several times if I didn't like it for what it cost me on the other website and I will still use that lady that makes my covers. She did excellent work; however, it was $320 versus 30 to 50 bucks. Now that is a big difference.

So if you have talent even the smallest of talent, you can list your service here. Perhaps you are good at proofreading or maybe grant writing, or help with math or science project, or you can do someone's grant. Maybe you're a teacher you can solve help people understand complex math problems, or you can help someone with their term paper. These are things that people will pay for okay it may not be a lot $5, $10, $20 may not be a lot, but it's a start, and a start is always a start. I know this was off topic but I wanted you to know about this resource, and maybe you can post your services and help you become financially independent also. Every little bit helps. I know this for sure.

Ok so I've told you everything that I think I can say to you about marketing and I'm sure forgot some things, I can also be sure that someone will send me a message and tell me what I forgot. They will point out that whatever I forgot is something that I really should have gone over. When this happens, I will be more than happy to include it and update the book and then mention in the book who told me of my error. I've been doing this for quite some time and become second nature to me so I may just forget something entirely and not think of it at all.

So if you think of something I missed then just drop me a line. I'll be happy to take care of it, and you're probably right. I may have overlooked something, but I am more than happy to make any adjustments. So just let me know when you read this, if you find something in marketing that you think I left out, let me know right away. Maybe you're better than I am at marketing. If so I will jump on it and take care of it right away. And send you a gift too!!

Chapter 25 Solving The Ultimate Problem

There's one big problem with Amazon, and it is the same as there with all other online retail stores. I did touch base with this subject in one other chapter here. But the problem here is more than just feedback and cheating or thieving customers. The ultimate problem is your customers. Customers are the problem. I know sometimes I too have been a problem to sellers. Not typically but I can be a problem.

Here the problem is your buyers, your customers. You will know them when they arrive, in the first contact you have from them you will understand who and what they are. These problem customers will complain because they didn't get there $1.35 item to them in the time they expected. Amazon will tell them that it's supposed to be there between will say the 10th and the 26 get it the next day. And when they don't get it the next day after they ordered, they will start complaining to Amazon that you didn't ship the product correctly. They didn't get it on time. When Amazon sees that you did get it there in time, they will ignore their complaint. And trust me, they will leave you negative feedback, and they will leave you a poor review. But if they do, you can contact Amazon and say look, it was there on time, they will see that and they will remove it. It's all okay.

So your customer is the ultimate problem, but also your customer is the ultimate solution. Without the customer, you have no reason to be on Amazon. If you looked at my feedback, you would see that 99% of the people love me, but that 1% just hates me and would like to kill me. They would want to make sure that I was never born, and that my family doesn't exist, and they will go out of their way to make your life miserable including creating new accounts just to buy things from you to leave negative feedback. I have had people do this so many times before so it will happen to you as well. So if your customer is your ultimate problem, then you need to come up with the ultimate solution.

What is the ultimate solution?

The ultimate solution is you, just like the customer is the ultimate problem. You are the ultimate solution; it is you who control your customers and not your customers who control you. You must face each customer with a happy and smile just as if it were natural to do. You must also do that with a nasty people. In fact, that hurts them more than you being nasty back to them.

So the ultimate solution is you. I will repeat it, and you must remember you must be the ultimate solution. I know this will be a problem for most people, especially since we all have egos. And trust me when I know that the customer is wrong and I know they're trying to scam me, I will have an issue with this. And even when I know I am right; I still have to go back to the adage that the customer is always right. Because they are the ones, which cause problems.

It is those screaming people; those nasty people are the ones who are going to tell everybody what a bad person you are. But those 3000 other nice people that you've done business with who are very happy with your services, so delighted that they love you will not cause you any problems. Why because they are happy. If they had a daughter, they would let you date her.

So those people are the ones who will make your life miserable. The keyword there is if you let them make your life miserable. The critical thing is that you just don't let them make your life miserable. You resolve not to let them get to you, and if you don't let them get to you, then it hurts them more than anything. If they are screaming and they are complaining they will be telling you that you've done wrong and would do this to you and would do this to you. It is easy because they are hiding behind their computer, up front and close they would run and hide.

I have had it happen over a $4 box of Staples, the staples this lady received were 1/4 of an inch too short. This was not my fault as the packet had the correct size on it. The manufacturer must have put them in the wrong box, or she measured it wrong. I don't know which it was, but her responses to me were how stupid I was. People like me shouldn't be allowed to have children. I should be in jail for this. And all of this for a $4 item. So some people no matter how much you do, are still going to be angry and will leave negative feedback. Maybe they will file an A-to-Z claim or file a chargeback.

Whatever it is and you just have to be the ultimate solution. Just smile and remember that if you are buying things from Liquidation.com, you aren't paying much for each item. I know it is a principle but calm down please and think about it. By the time you figure it all out even if it's a $70 item, by the time you pay for shipping your cost is low that It is unbelievable.

So in the end that $70 item cost you about $3. It still hurts. But it is only your pride that is hurting not your pocket. So think of it like that you're just losing $3. If you get angry, this person wins. They will hurt you by leaving feedback or an A-Z claim and all over nothing. Are you willing to lose your Amazon account over an idiot?

The critical thing to remember is this now this person knows he's an idiot because he's acting this way. He must know he is an idiot. And now you know he's an idiot because he's acted this way to you. Therefore you see you both agree on something you both agree that he's an idiot. Now you can live peacefully with that, and you can live happily with this idea. Now you become the ultimate solution to the ultimate problem. Customers being the ultimate problem and you being the ultimate solution by just smiling back at them.

No matter how nasty they are, no matter how many times they call you stupid things, just tell them you're sorry saying and you understand how they feel. Even though you probably really don't care, but this will hurt them more than anything in the world. They may continue to scream and yell, but if you continue to aggravate them, they will make your life miserable.

Remember some of these people have nothing better to do than to go on and make complaints about you. They may go on the bulletin board to make complaints or go on and buy new things just to screw you up because they have nothing better to do. But if you don't let them get into your skin, then they can't get ahead of you. You just don't let them bother you, and they will do what most worms do. Yes, I think they are worms. And as worms, they will crawl back under a rock someplace, and they'll forget about you. They will go on about their daily life being a worm happy that they stole something from someone.

But as you know Karma is a bitch as you know. God sees everything. So everything they do bad nasty will come back to get them. You just don't have the do it. Karma will get them, or God will get them. So live peacefully and be the ultimate solution to the ultimate problem. If you can do this, then your time on Amazon or any venue will be good

Chapter 26 Insider Tips

The best insider tip I can tell you about Amazon is that when Amazon sends you an email, you answer within an hour or two hours. You don't wait the three days that they allow you, you explain it right up front. More importantly, whatever Amazon sends you, have about three sentences to catch their attention. So your best thing is to answer their questions in the first three sentences.

And those may be all the chance you have to get the attention of the person reading your email. Whether it be seller performance, whether it be an A-to-Z claim or chargeback you have three sentences. So your first three sentences don't need to be "I think this buyer was a real loser and he's just trying to scam me, and I think this is unfair. If you do this and then you start to explain what happened.", you will not get an answer.

I have helped people with accounts that have been closed for months with no answer from seller support. These people showed me their emails. They were sending messages to seller support but explaining their problem more than halfway down the paragraph. But what they're doing just won't work. Amazon gets too many emails, the need to get their point across quickly to get any help or understanding.

Amazon needs to see the first three sentences tell them the story. Amazons employees have been trained for this. I've talked to them personally. I've spoken to Amazon seller reps personally outside of Amazon. They tell me that if you don't make your point within the first three sentences, you will get no help. Amazon wants you to admit to your problem. Even if you're not wrong if you don't acknowledge that you had a performance problem you will fail. If you don't admit you had late shipping or you don't accept that chargeback problem even though it's not your fault. If you don't admit it in the first three sentences and get their attention, then they will skip right over and go to the next person. So you need to acknowledge this up front. Example here.

Here's an example. "Yes, thank you for letting me know that my seller performance is below standard. I understand my rating of my ODR is 2.3%. I know this and I have come up with a plan to resolve this issue." In these three sentences, you told them and admitted to YOUR problem. You thanked them for letting you know, and you acknowledged the problem. And lastly you have a plan to fix this, and you did it in all three sentences. You told them everything they needed know.

Now you can explain your plan. You tell Amazon your plan of action and how you intend to do this. There you can explain that in fact, the customer tried to scam me. However, I've taken more aggressive steps to reach out to customers to try to resolve their issues. I am working hard to make them more understand the Amazon and the online selling process. I am also going to be more proactive with my refunds and more aggressive in reaching out to customers. I want to see if I can resolve their issues up front before becomes a problem where Amazon has to get involved. We apologize Amazon had to get involved in such a trivial thing.

You can add you are also going to start sending letters and notes with each one of our purchases giving them a direct phone number to your customer service line. Whether you have one or not, it doesn't matter. You tell them you do and that you're going to take care of these issues. If you don't, that's your problem, and it will haunt you. You should have a direct number that you know when that phone rings, that it is a customer from online sales.

That's just excellent customer service. I can't tell you how happy I am when I get a letter from someone in the box saying, hey we think we've done everything right but if you have any questions or comments, please give us a call. We will do our best to resolve the issue. Thank you. Wow, you just made me happy, and if I do have a problem, the first thing I will do is call you and not Amazon, because you reached out to me already.

These tips alone will save your Amazon account, especially if you do them proactively. This means you need to do them before you have a problem before you have an issue. If you send these little notices out to everyone and email people to make sure they're happy you will be better than your competition.

Also if for some reason you can't ship an item then buy it from someone else. If I could show you my personal Amazon account, you would see that I have purchased hundreds of items from Amazon or other sellers to fix an issue. That's just excellent customer service. Why? I want to make sure my customers happy. I want to make sure my customer is taken care of very well. If you do this, then your customers will appreciate it. Keep in mind there are sometimes when your inventory is wrong, or you find something is broken, fix the issue first, be proactive. You take care these issues right up front right, and they don't come problems later.

Being proactive is your saving grace when it comes to Amazon or when it comes to any online or at any retail marketplace. How many times have you called in with a problem and the first rep you talk to said sorry there is nothing I can do for you. But when you talk to someone else there at the same company, they say don't worry sir I'll take care that for you. You are the person that says I'll take care that for you, sir.

Think about it, when it happens to you, you are thrilled and love the fact this person fixed the issue for you. You be that person, and your customers will love you. You need only stand up and take care of them up front first. If you do that, you will have good feedback, you will have good customers, you will be proactive, and you won't have any problems on Amazon.

People say they get banned from Amazon a lot and yes I've been banned a couple of times myself. But I send in my appeal and Amazon puts me back on. Most the time it is just a misunderstanding. Sometimes it's my sloppy work. I should've gotten pulled off Amazon because I was careless. Once I have fixed those errors, I make sure that I

don't do them again. In the past six years, I have not been
pulled off of Amazon once. I honestly thought when I first
started out that they do that every 60 days just to get you. I
was pulled off within 30 days for one thing then I was
pulled off for selling too many items too quickly.

I was also pulled off for so many little things that I
thought wow at least every 60 days this happens. They just
pull you off and make you send them a message to figure
out what you're doing wrong. Then you appeal, and you get
back on Amazon and start selling again. I thought that was
the procedure I did know I was just making that many
screw ups. Once I realized I was making so many screw-
ups, I stopped. I now no longer make those screw ups.

Therefore, in six years I haven't been pulled off once
since I cleaned up my act. You don't want to make these
mistakes again this is merely a good business practice. So
be proactive, be clean and treat other people the way you
want to be treated yourself. As far as Amazon goes as just
simple yet no worries sleep well at night.

Chapter 27 Bonus: Winning The Buy Box

To sell on Amazon and really be successful you need to capture the buy box. You can try to do this manually but it is tedious or purchase software which will automate the process. Please check the links in the back of this book for my favorite choices for this software.

More than 78% of all sales on Amazon are made through the buy box. Quite simply when you search any item on Amazon, and you click the buy it now, that was a buy box sale. It makes it easy for sellers and buyers. If you click the list of items below the description, you may see many items that are listed, in prices above and below the buy box price. Some people will look for the best price this way. Others simply search and then click buy. It's that easy, and if you capture the buy box, then your item sells.

When you look at the sales page, there may be fifty items listed, but only one will capture the much-desired buy box. On the Amazon detail page, there are typically three to four other sellers whose items are listed on the right. Most people do not see this and will click buy it now. Bing!! you just made a sale IF you had the buy box.

Now the buy box is almost always not the best price. In fact most of the times it is higher than the lowest price. Through some amazing algorithm which is a secret of Amazon, the item and seller meeting all the requirements gets that position. Manually you can do it, but it is challenging. I use software to achieve this. Sometimes the software lowers the price and other times it raises the price. The software can be set up for capturing only the buy box

Many times when you analyze the items, the cheaper options come out more expensive without the free shipping of the prime option. The normal way Amazon lists items is with the price plus shipping, and this will affect the buy box. However a sellers ODR, which we discussed earlier and his POP or perfect order percentage, significantly affect whether any particular seller gets the buy box it is not price alone. Your selling feedback must be above 90%, and you're in stock rate must be close to 100%. Amazon and customers hate when you sell an item and run out of stock. It disappoints customers and angry upset customers hurt all sellers.

Strangely enough Amazons ODR must be awful as their feedback is below 87% at the time of this writing. If that were you or me, we would have been suspended by now. But I guess you can't suspend yourself from your own store. See what I mean by being your own boss. No matter how bad you do something you can't get fired.

One thing to always keep in mind when trying to get the buy box is that lowering the price is not always the best business practice. First, you lose money, and you can start a downward spiral until one of you sells the item you have. Then the other seller makes money selling to another customer at a MUCH higher price.

Stay calm and let your hard work or let the software do its job. Just stay calm, and don't get frustrated.

Chapter 28 Multiple Streams Of Income

Now that you have Amazon down to a science and you probably can do this in your sleep. And that's a good thing. But to be secure in life what you need to do is have other sources of income. You need to protect your way of life and your family. I realized this once I was pushed out of the corporate job that I'd had for more than 15 years. I decided I would no longer work for one company and I would never be a slave to someone. I would now be my own master; I would be my own boss.

You need to decide what you want. Do you continue to work for someone and let them make all the money off of your hard work? Or do you want to do the hard work yourself, and make money for yourself? The one good thing I can tell you about working for yourself is that if I want to take time off to go fishing with my son, I can. If I want to take off time to go skiing with my daughter, I can. I recently took my daughter Hawaii. Want to know why? Because we could, and we had the time to be together.

I'm not bragging to tell you this to show you how much money I've made. In fact, if you knew I was sitting on the beach recording, this might make you little irritated. But I am sitting on the beach in front of my house recording this as you read this. I'm probably wasting time, but I have multiple streams of income. I have other streams of income. I have books; I have sales on other websites, I have sales on eBay.

You need to read my eBay book to find out how to set up a good eBay account. And how to protect yourself from eBay so that they don't catch you having multiple accounts. Because they again don't like anyone to have multiple accounts. Yes, they say you can have more than one, but when they find out, they find some way to cancel you. Trust me I had 15,000 feedbacks on one account, and they canceled that account because they said I was manipulating the system. How was I manipulating the system? I wasn't doing anything except selling stuff, but they canceled the account anyway. And they canceled another one with a thousand feedback. I have fifteen eBay accounts, and I use them all the with same computers that I use for Amazon. So pick up a copy of my eBay book. It will be out at the same time you find this one, that will tell you how to go with eBay and how to make a living on eBay as well.

There are many ways you can have multiple streams of income again. I said I would never put all my eggs in one basket. Because I got hurt that away, I got burned badly. Had I not been in this position where I was at and knew the things that I knew I probably would not be doing this right now. I would still be searching for a job, hoping to find something mid-level management or maybe even fall back down to sales again. But because I had a good analytical background, I was able to pull this out of thin air and succeed. And then write a book to help you, so you don't make the same mistakes I did. Now you can benefit from my success and my mistakes.

Now I'm not saying that I'm a super success, but I have done well considering where I started. But honestly, I would love to hear from now. I would like to have you to email me and tell me, hey Bruce I sold more stuff than you did in two days than you ever sold the month. If so I'll be happy. I want to sit down and hear how you did it, and maybe even write a book on how you did so other people can learn how to do it.

Next, I will bet you are wondering if I'm making so much money, why would I tell people how to do this? Because this is another stream of income in my life, yes I am honest about this. If I teach you how to do this if maybe you will want some personal coaching from me.

Maybe you will want me to help you set up the accounts. I'll do that, and I'll log into your computer from a remote location. I'll go through the motions, and I'll help you do that, and yes I charge for that. It's my time, but I can save you the time so that you don't have problems. Why? Because I've been selling on Amazon for so long, I can do it in my sleep. Once you see me do it, you'll be able to do it just as fast and accurate.

I want you to do it once, after that, you'll be able to do it twice, three times, four times. It is no problem. Multiple streams of income are what make you a success. I can be lying here on the beach relaxing and enjoying myself and still make money. I can be golfing and still make money. I can be on vacation, and I still make money, knowledge is king. Once you learn how to do this, you can teach people in your area how to sell things. You could also put out advertisements on Craigslist saying that you will sell their items on Amazon and split the profit. Now people bring you things to sell. You only need to advertise and ship them when they sell. Wow, free inventory!! You never had to lay out a cent to buy the things, and if it doesn't sell, you have not lost anything. Amazon doesn't charge you when you list something only when you sell the item.

Keep in mind with an Amazon and a couple of eBay accounts if you get one account closed you still have income. Why because you have money coming in on other accounts. Other situations can help also. So whether your additional stream of income is your current job or whether your other stream of income is a part-time job you still have money. Maybe another stream of income is selling information. Perhaps there is something you know that other people will pay for that knowledge.

This relates to Amazon because you can sell books about your knowledge. Just like I'm selling you this book on my knowledge. I have more than 70 books on Amazon under various pen names. Some are selling the information that I have learned through my school of hard knocks. This information will make you smarter and make you more successful. I have a college degree, but it never made me as much money as I've made selling things on Amazon. Selling books and selling my knowledge about the things I've learned through the hard way. I'm sure there's something out there that you know better than anyone. And you can do this just like I'm doing it right now.

I have a hobby of ham radio. With my ham radio, I know how to build antennas, install radios, and find noise solutions to get rid of the noise in my receiver. I can do this better than most people, better than most other hams that also can do it. But there are people out there starting up that don't know how to do this. So I can sell my knowledge to teach them how to do these things.

This is another stream of income that you can start right now. If you sit back, you can think about it you could be too late. What do you know well? In fact, let's do a little do a little quiz or a project right now, grab a piece of paper and set down in a quiet area. Write down your hobbies, write down something that you know very well. Write down your work, and it doesn't matter if you're a dishwasher or whatever, you know secrets that we don't know.

I have a detailer at my wife's car dealership. This man taught me so much. I've learned things from detailers of cars that are amazing. I know a way to repair carpet in the car that I would never have even considered. But this guy is just a hard-working man who didn't make a lot of money. Yet, he taught me so much. I still tell people about how smart this guy was at least in that field. He may not have a college degree, but he knows how to do things that I wouldn't even think of how to do.

And I'm sure there are things there that you know that I couldn't even imagine. You want to use this knowledge to get into the multiple streams of income If you have an idea then email me. I now own a publishing company, and I will help you get your book published. Then you can start on a successful road with your life. Be truthful with your knowledge, knowledge is king but use your actual knowledge. I know someone who outsourced their information to a guy online. They didn't check the info, and they ended up getting banned for lifetime. Plagiarism. They are banned for life from Amazon and two other online book sellers.

So he's banned for life. But yes I did fix him up. I did get him onto another account with another online seller, and they are selling his books on Amazon. He was able to start all over and start fresh. I taught him some tricks, and now he has books for sale under many pen names. Yes, there are ways to get around everything. I will show you that, I can show you how to get your books published how to get your book to market smartly. You can email me directly, and I'll help you through it, or you can buy my book.

You don't have to this; I'm merely telling you that there is a book available. I have published a book on how to get your book published without any help from anyone except yourself. It's not as hard as you think it's not rocket science especially if could do it. I'm not the smartest kid on the block. I work hard for everything that I have learned and why am I telling you all this? Because I want to see my knowledge passed on to someone else. I don't want all my knowledge wasted and gone forever. I want someone in 30 years now to say this guy taught me how to make money. And then I will live on through my knowledge. But only if you will USE IT!!!

I know I've gone on here for a long time about nothing. And yes, this is the end of the book, but if you feel you need some personal coaching, then you can email me. You have my email address and if not it is in the very back of the book. It is also on the first page of the book; you can email me that's my private email addresses. Yes, of course, I have multiple personal email addresses, but I will answer you. I only respond email once a day, usually in the morning, so you email me your questions, and I'll answer. If you need personal help setting up your account, you email me I'll do that for you. Yes, I don't do that for free because it does take time out of my day, but is not expensive. If you need help and have hit a roadblock, I will help.

I will help you get started, and I will help you get it done. See I've done this so many times it becomes second nature to me. After you have done it a few times and will be the same way for you too. You won't even think about it. I'm sure that you're with a job right now, you have tasks and can do the same thing. So I'm not any smarter than you. I did this already, and I can teach you how to do it. I can help you get through it and once you get through this., you'll be an expert too.

Chapter 29 Motivation

The best motivation is your wife and children, look at them and then say I can't fail. I will not fail. I will succeed. I must succeed.

Now for some motivational talk. A lot of things I want to tell you may not make sense. They don't make sense to because you're not living this life yet. And you have not experienced the things I have laid out. But let me tell you if you don't do the things that I have laid out here, you will fail. Now, this doesn't mean you'll fail completely. But I've given you a path in this book to follow if you don't follow the path you will fail. At least you will fail in the way that I'm trying to teach you how to do things.

Now I may not be the best teacher for you. You may want to find someone else to teach you. But my way does work. I know it works. I've done it time and time again. I'm showing people how to do it, I've talked about it. I've had seminars with people that have paid me $1000 a person to teach them this system privately. It works, and if you follow the methods I have laid out then you can have multiple businesses and have multiple streams of income

I can't tell you what or how much well you will succeed. But I can tell you that all you have to do is try. If you try and you fail, that doesn't mean you're a failure. If you have followed my system, then you will have learned something. And if you fail, then you have learned not to go this way. Step back and try a different way. When I made mistakes, I learned what not to do. It made me stronger and better. I have laid out all those failures here. If you come across a roadblock then email me, perhaps I can help.

That's what this entire book is about, overcoming failure. My failure will become your success. There are two types of failure. The kind of failure where you make a mistake and learn from it. And the kind where you make the same mistake over and over. Usually, you make a mistake once or twice, and you realize your mistake, and you learn from it. If you are the latter, then you need to stop and think about your process and fix it. If you can recognize this failure, then you can fix it.

You think you didn't learn anything right? But you did learn what you're not supposed to do. If you do it once or twice and you learn from it. Realize I made a stupid mistake and then move on. This is like the little child that when you tell them that the pan is hot and they still put their hand out to touch it. What happens then? They don't touch the pan again. They don't go back and say I don't think that was hot enough and try it again. This doesn't mean you're a failure; it just means that you learned something.

As long as you take it that away, then it is the best way to learn. Nobody was born knowing all this information. Trust me, that's why I'm telling you all this information that's in this book and sharing with you all my knowledge so you can learn my failures. I failed so many times I wanted to give up. I thought I would never get it if I had given up. I probably back at some job, some boring job in someplace just waiting for them to tell me you're no longer working here. Then I would be stuck, but no I had a family, I didn't give up. I knew I could do it. I had faith in myself, and I knew that just because I made a screw-up or I made a mistake doesn't mean I was a failure.

The act of trying but not succeeding does not mean you're a failure. But the action of not trying and saying I couldn't do it even though you never tried that's a failure. You will fail before you ever start and you will learn nothing. All you learned was to teach yourself that you're a failure and that's the wrong thing to do.

Would you do that to a child, would you say there's no way you can ever learn that just stop. You're going to be stupid the rest your life. Just forget about your never going to learn how to do those math problems don't even try to, play some ball or play some video games. Would you ever do that? No, but you we do it continuously to ourselves.

So if you can get to the point where you can get it through your head that failure is not trying. Then you will win. If you can get it through your head what failure is, then you're not going to be a failure you're going to be a success in one way or another. Learning from your mistakes is the best knowledge you can have. I can tell you all these things, and hopefully, you'll avoid the mistakes that I have made, but if you make a mistake yourself, that's when you're really going to learn. You will say damn, he was right. I shouldn't have done that and now I know what's right. And now you know that this is the wrong way to do things. Hopefully, you will learn from what I have told you here, and if you by some chance make a mistake and end up taking a different route, you'll figure it out.

As I've said numerous times whether you follow my method, someone else's method, or create your own method and decide to go against everything just like I did, you can succeed. The fact that you want to succeed, the fact that you believe you can succeed is your most significant strength. I know this all this motivational stuff is probably a little mushy for everybody here but the bottom line is its reality. The reality is you are you're worst enemy. If you set yourself up for failure, you will fail. If you set yourself up for high hopes, and then you say I wanted to make $10,000, but I only made $3000, you will say wow, what a loser I am. You just told yourself you are a failure.

But if you set yourself up for a reasonable goal and you get close to that goal then you will feel you succeeded. Failure will always be there in your mind, but damn you went from nothing to $3000. Maybe you didn't make the $10,000 you were wanting, but you went from no money to $3000 in sales. Wow, that's a success. To start with nothing and go on to make something out of it is powerful. If you took $150 worth of products that you bought, clean them up, advertise, list them and sell them for $1000 profit. That's a success to me.

You can do this, and it may not be because my book helped you but because you are motivated to succeed. This has nothing to do with the rest of the book in all reality. However, the matter of the fact is that you need to believe in yourself. You probably have heard it time and time again, but you do need to believe in yourself. If you think you're going to fail, then you're going to fail because you don't have anything to believe in. Believe in yourself, and remember to go for what you can and do the best you can. That's all that anyone can do.

You're only a failure if you sit back and say I can't do this and you never try. That makes you a failure in my book. If you fail at something, then you can try again. The important thing is you tried. That's the best anyone can ask from you. You will do better next time. Why? Because you learned what went wrong this time. You learned what you need to do and you learned what you did wrong. That's a success in my book.

You don't consider your failure when you go to school, and you don't know the answers, do you? No, of course not, you need to be taught. Consider this as your learning by going to school. You are learning something you know nothing about. And just because you can't do it today doesn't mean you're going to fail. Learn from my mistakes and yours.

I am not a motivational speaker, but I can tell you that's the absolute God's truth. If you believe in yourself, you're going to succeed. And if you believe you're going to fail and you told yourself you're going to fail then the honest truth is that you will fail. So the bottom line is, believe in yourself and failure is only a state of mind. Do your best always, and you will succeed. You may not do the best the first time; I know I sure as heck didn't. But if I had given up, I wouldn't be here today, and I would have abandoned all hope.

There is one last thing that I would like to tell you. If you learn nothing from this book, and I mean nothing, but you take away only what I've said in this chapter and you remember the fact that if you try, and you fail, and then you try again, you will have learned something. Now that is a real success.

Remember as Thomas Edison said "I have not failed. I've just found 10,000 ways that won't work." This is so true, live by it and take this with you the rest of your life.

Chapter 30 Final Thoughts

I hope you've enjoyed this book; I hope it's been something that has been beneficial to you. I've certainly enjoyed writing it. If you want to create multiple streams of income, then read my eBay book. This book tells you how to avoid eBay catches and pitfalls. I show you how to deal with customers and how to deal with problems that arise on eBay. It will also help you market your inventory on eBay. Also, I'll show you how to create multiple accounts on eBay using the same computers that you already have. This keeps you from having all your eggs in one basket. If something happens to your Amazon account, then you still have several accounts on eBay to run to and make money from,

Trust me some things sell on eBay that will never sell on Amazon. And some things will sell on Amazon that you couldn't give away on eBay. They are two different types of customers with two different mindset's. Personally, when I look for things for myself, I know what to look for on the Amazon, and I know what to look for on eBay. I'm sure you do too. There are certain things you think about automatically going to Amazon.

I also have additional books in this series. These books will tell you how to get started on other websites such as Google, Etsy, and Walmart. Or maybe you want to create an e-commerce website for your benefit. I can teach you how to start your own used car lot. I can also show you through my many other books and training courses on how to become an independent writer. Or how to become a blogger and make money from your blogging. I have a blogging book it is not very long, and it's very inexpensive. But it will give you all the essentials you need to learn about blogging. Several of my blogs have over 50,000 followers. And all I have to do is place one or two advertisements on them and boom I have sales. These people trust me, they know me, these people are part of my inner circle.

And again if you have questions about this book, you will have my email. I do answer all my emails, and I only give this email out to people buying my books. So when you send an email, it will come directly to me. I usually answer my emails only once a day, typically in the morning sometimes in the evening. So if you email me at 8 AM and I've done my email already for the morning, you will not hear from me until the next day. Don't get worried that I didn't get your email. It doesn't mean you need to email me three or four times. Some people will do this when they don't hear back from me. I'm telling you right away that I only email once a day and you need to learn to do that as well. It's a real time saver for you. You don't realize how much time you spend checking your emails.

Most people are checking their phone every five minutes looking to see if they have new emails. You need to relax. Even though sales are important, people aren't jumping on you right away. So relax. Take your time slow down. Slow down and do things right, take your time everything will get done and on time. When you speed up, you make mistakes. I'm telling you what you already know, you know I am right when you speed up you will make mistakes.

Take your time do things slowly but accurately, If you do sloppy work to get done you will most likely have to do it again. Maybe it will take you two or three times. Take your time, do it right the first time that way you don't have to come back again and start all over. Once you have done it right the first time, you'll be more likely to do it right the next time. Sloppy habits equal sloppy work. So if you get into the habit of doing something sloppy you will do it sloppy every time. Then you have to come back and clean up, and it makes a mess.

Get yourself into a routine. Get yourself into a routine that you do every day, and once you do it you will follow through, and it will become a habit. My routine is I get up, and then I go to my computer. I turn it on, and I take a shower. I start up some hot chocolate. I'm not a coffee person. I sit back down at my desk, and I read all my emails, then I answer them. After that, I head out to my warehouse to do my Amazon and my eBay and my other websites. Once I've completed that task and get everybody going to where they're going I am off on my own again.

Sometimes I take a drive my car and drive. Sometimes I'll drive 100 miles or so for the peace and quiet. It's a good environment and a great studio in my car. No distractions, well, not many. I don't have my phone on to bother me because I turned off. And I don't answer emails all day. And once I leave my office, my people, know not to call me unless it's an emergency. Don't call me I'm busy. I do my podcasts most the time from my car because I can drive to a beautiful scenic point here on the beach, relax and watch the waves. Then I sit back and enjoy myself with my nice cup of hot chocolate.

Develop your routine and once you develop a routine follow it every day. No matter what it is, follow the routine.

It helps keep you motivated. Even if it' getting up and going directly to your computer and answering your emails and then going to get something to eat. That's a routine do it every day don't deviate once you deviate it's not a habit. You need to make it something you know you're supposed to do, and you'll do it. You need to make it a habit. Habits become things you do autonomously. You don't even think about it that's what you need to make this into a habit, good habits make good sales and make good people.

One final thought here, none of the things I've told you in this book are rocket science. This is all stuff that you can quickly learn on your own. You don't need anybody to hold your hand. The only thing I've done is I've put the information together in a great format. It's easy for you to do and it's easy for you to do this and go along step-by-step. I believe if you follow the step-by-step instructions on how to do things you will succeed. I have put things here in an easy to follow format. I have tried to make things easy so you can avoid the pitfalls I had.

I am trying to prevent you from having any problems. All you need to do is follow the steps one by one. Work through the steps, and you'll find yourself successful. Now you may not find yourself as successful as you expected to be in the period you wanted. However, persistence will make you a lot more successful than you would be if you sat around and did nothing.

Trust me I will point out to you as if I didn't get through to you that I'm not a genius. I'm certainly not a rocket scientist. I may know a little bit more about marketing than the average person. I may know more about Amazon than the average person. Nothing I have done here is going to stand me out as a genius. It's hard work and experience that has made me the person I am today. And it will make you the same way in one year or two years also. But again this depends on how quick you have you are on your learning curve.

That's all it takes is for you to learn. Once you learn it you will become a genius too; you will eat, sleep, drink and dream about it as I sometimes do myself. Unfortunately, I can't have ordinary dreams, but hey it is what it is. This system requires your perseverance and for you to work at it. If you think you're going to step back and this is going to come to you, then think again. If so, then go back to the convenience store or back to your checkout line and be the clerk that you always wanted to be. Because that's where you will end up, right back where you started. With this program, you have to work at it. (that four letter work again!) Anything valuable in life will require you have to work at it.

But with this system, if you follow through with it, you will be able to make something out of it. You will be able to do something and build a successful business. I have, and I did it from nothing all while not being the sharpest tool in the shed. I'm sure some of you people out there are probably way sharper than I am. You may be able to do it with a lot more ease than I did.

Once again thank you for reading my book. I hope you've learned something from reading this book. Please click the rating here on your Kindle and give me a five-star rating if you liked the book. If you didn't, then please email me and tell me why you didn't like it. What you think I should add? What do you think I should change? I'll be happy to do whatever changes the majority of the people would like. If there's something you think I forgot or something, I have missed then email me and tell me about it. And if you have questions about something that you think I didn't go over in-depth enough email me. I'll respond to you. I'll help you get it done.

Thank you, and I hope you enjoyed it and good fortune to you on Amazon.

So my last words in this chapter are to GO FOR IT!!

Appendix

Wholesale sources

http://www.liquidation.com/

http://www.globalsources.com/

http://www.bstock.com/

https://www.wholesalecentral.com/

https://www.dhgate.com/

https://www.made-in-china.com

https://www.alibaba.com/

https://www.aliexpress.com/

http://www.govliquidation.com/

http://www.auctionzip.com/liquidation.html

https://www.onlineliquidationauction.com/

https://liquidations.walmart.com/

https://www.usauctiononline.com/

Trade Shows

http://www.globalsources.com/

https://10times.com/

http://www.expodatabase.com/trade-shows-america/usa/ase

https://www.absoluteexhibits.com/top-100-usa-shows/

http://eventsinamerica.com/

https://www.tradefairdates.com/

Companies who will appeal to Amazon on your behalf

https://www.amazonappeal.com/

https://www.amazonappealletters.com/

https://theamazonappeal.com/

https://www.amazonsellerprotection.com

https://sellercare.com/

A-Z claim letter

Thank you for taking the time to read my appeal.

First I take full responsibility for the A-Z claim. I realize that not being attentive as I should to my customers has resulted in the suspension of my account. I have constructed a plan below to alleviate this problem in the future. We want to make sure we adhere to the high quality standards that the Amazon name implies. We value Amazon and the customers that Amazon provides.

My Plan of action:

We have reviewed all of Amazon's guidelines to ensure that we are fully compliant in all aspects. We have also decided that monthly we will again review the policies for any changes to be sure we are 100% compliant in the future.

Below we have addressed the problems which caused our suspension.

Quality:

I have suspended all sales to reevaluate my entire inventory. Once completed I will also test all items before shipping to make sure everything works well. I will also make sure all items match the item listing precisely before shipping to avoid customer dissatisfaction.

Speed:

I intend to upgrade all future sales to the next level of shipping at no cost. I will send out every order within 24 hours of the order being placed. This will result in higher customer satisfaction. We have also added extra packing to all items to ensure any package shipped will not arrive with damage.

A-Z complaints:

Effective today I have started a campaign of contacting the customer when the order ships and when it arrive. I have given each customer my direct contact information via my business card enclosed in each shipped package. I have directed those customers to contact me directly. I have found that most A-Z claims are as a result of customer and seller miscommunication. This should alleviate this problem in the future.

Here at (your store name), we strive to satisfy all customers, while we know that it is impossible to please everyone, we will do our best to achieve 100%.

We do hope this has addressed all our issues. We look forward to serving our valued Amazon customers as quickly as possible. Please reinstate our account as I can assure you this is a one-time occurrence.

Thank You.
(Your Name)
(Your Phone Number)

Feedback letter

Thank you for taking the time to read my appeal.

First I take full responsibility for the high ODR rate. I realize that not being attentive as I should to my customers has resulted in the suspension of my account. I have constructed a plan below to alleviate this problem in the future. We want to make sure we adhere to the high quality standards that the Amazon name implies. We value Amazon and the customers that Amazon provides.

My Plan of action:

We have reviewed all of Amazon's guidelines to ensure that we are fully compliant in all aspects. We have also decided that monthly we will again review the policies for any changes to be sure we are 100% compliant in the future. Below we have addressed the problems which caused our suspension.

Quality:

I have suspended all sales to reevaluate my entire inventory. Once completed I will also test all items before shipping to make sure everything works well. I will also make sure all items match the item listing precisely before shipping to avoid customer dissatisfaction.

Speed:

I intend to upgrade all future sales to the next level of shipping at no cost. I will send out every order within 24 hours of the order being placed. This will result in higher customer satisfaction. We have also added extra packing to all items to ensure any package shipped will not arrive with damage.

Integrity:

Effective today I have started a campaign of contacting the customer when the order ships and when it arrive. I have given each customer my direct contact information via my business card enclosed in each shipped package. I have directed those customers to contact me directly. I have found that most claims are as a result of customer and seller miscommunication. This should alleviate this problem in the future.

Buyers are receiving orders that are defective:

I will make sure to personally test out everything before I add it to my Amazon inventory so that buyers will have a good experience. I want to make sure even the new items are tested for 100% compliance and working order. We will also recheck upon shipping to verify that it is in working shape and not torn, dented or damaged in any way.

I will also in the future either refund a customer or replace the items at the first instance of any issue. We want our customers to be satisfied with our products and services; We do not doubt that this measure alone will significantly improve our customer relations.

Here at (your store name), we strive to satisfy all customers, while we know that it is impossible to please everyone, we will do our best to achieve 100%.

We do hope this has addressed all our issues. We look forward to serving our valued Amazon customers as quickly as possible. Please reinstate our account as I can assure you this is a one-time occurrence.

Thank You.
   (Your Name)
(Your Phone Number)

General appeal letter

Use the above letters and modify if any suspension notice arrives that is not one of the two above. These are the most common and why I addressed these alone.

Email me direct at Bep@c-4.net

I will reply within 24 hours!

Printed in Great Britain
by Amazon

37938083R00142